A BRIEF
HISTORY
of TREES

'Queen Victoria's Tree', Windsor Great Park, 1894.

A BRIEF
HISTORY
of TREES

Gertrude Briggs

First published in the United Kingdom in 2016
Published by Max Press, London

10 9 8 7 6 5 4 3 2 1

Text © 2016 by Gertrude Briggs
Design and layout © 2016 by Max Press

ISBN: 978 1 906251 789

Printed by CPI UK, Chatham, Kent

CONTENTS

INTRODUCTION

From sweet chestnut trees planted by Alexander the Great to fossils of great oaks dating back to the Interglacial period 300,000 years ago, trees have played a central role in mankind's myths and religions since antiquity, and have been given deep and sacred meanings throughout the world. Trees stand between heaven and earth, associated with creation as well as the underworld, protectors and providers that offer fruit, medicine and guard against the elements and evil spirits.

Human beings, observing the annual growth, death and revival of their foliage, have always seen regarded these remarkable feats of nature as powerful symbols of death and rebirth. Evergreen trees such as the yew tree have long been regarded as symbols of the eternal, planted in sites that have been regarded as sacred long before churches or monasteries shared the same ground.

This brief history includes those trees that have made a special contribution to humanity. You will find among these pages trees that have defined our communities and have become intertwined with our values, as well as those that have featured in language, history, art, religion, politics, and even social structure. Their wood has provided products from paper and building materials, food and beverages to costumes and musical instruments. Their bark and leaves have provided medicine before the development of commercial drugs.

Trees were revered in the ancient world and ever since many have been seen as holy. Although religion has treated the worship of trees as idolatry, certain trees have developed a rich symbolism and have become inextricably linked with beliefs, such as the holly tree in Christianity, with its sharp thorns and red berries, and the olive tree, regarded as a blessing in Islam. Frankincense, neem and myrrh trees are regarded as sites of pilgrimages, places of ritual and the recital of prayers. Wreaths, ribbons or rags are suspended to win blessings for sick humans or livestock, or for good luck.

In mythology, trees are portrayed as ancestral symbols of wisdom, authority and custom, providing a bond between the dead and the living. Trees have been regarded as sources of good and evil, power and protection. The tree has power to give life and rebirth as well as to bring about death. In Gaelic and Celtic mythology certain trees such as the elder, hawthorn and the elder have been associated with magic more than others; whereas in ancient Greek mythology apple and fig trees have occupied centre-stage, renowned for their rich symbolism.

Trees have also been instrumental in advancing mankind's pioneering adventures across our planet. The China fir, originally discovered by botanist Allan Cunningham and introduced to Europe in 1802 by plant hunter Robert Fortune, is a testament to the great age of global exploration in the eighteenth and nineteenth centuries when many species, including the extraordinary handkerchief, spotted by a French missionary living in China, somehow made their way across the world, often despite treacherous seafaring conditions.

Some tree discoveries have proved crucial to scientific advances. The chinchona, for example, produces quinine, still today the basis of many anti-malarial drugs. Lemons and oranges were found to contain high quantities of vitamin C that led to the discovery of scurvy as well as its cure. The neem is believed to cure so many ailments that it has been renamed in some parts of India as the 'village pharmacy'. Other trees have played a crucial role in international trade, creating international commercial empires, inspiring political disputes and battles for millennia. Coffee, cacao and spice trees such as nutmeg, mace, cinnamon produced fruit that from the earliest ages formed vital links between East and West. Silk owes its discovery thanks to the mulberry tree.

In some regions trees have even served judicial roles. They can represent mediators or decision makers. They are physical boundary markers that define property and provide evidence of rights in judicial disputes, a symbol of friendship and feature in all festive occasions. Among the Igbo of Southern Nigeria, for example, all discussions, prayers, and ceremonies begin with the breaking of cola nuts.

No wonder trees have provided inspiration for poets and artists down the ages, from the elm that inspired Alfred, Lord Tennyson to describe a heady summer's day in the countryside, to the swaying cypresses captured by Vincent van Gogh's genius. They are an integral part of who we are and this small tome is a celebration of their magnificence.

'Wellingtonia at Penrhyn Castle',
from *A Dictionary of Universal Knowledge*, 1880.

ACACIA

ACACIAS ARE COMMONLY known as thorn trees. Their English name originates from the ancient Greek *akakia*, ακακία, a term used by Theophrastus and Dioscorides to denote thorn trees, meaning thorn or point.

Acacias belong to the legume or pea family, and thrive in the arid wastes of the Middle East, Africa, Australia and South America. They survive in hot, dry climates because as the desert people say, they have their 'head in the sun but their feet in water'. Their roots have nitrogen-fixing nodules that allow them to grow in poor, sandy soil and with little rainfall.

The acacia, or *shittim* in Hebrew, is also known as the *Acacia nilotica*, literally 'from the Nile', or *A. seyal*, derived from the Arabic word for 'torrent' on account of the fact that they are often to be found in *oueds* or dry riverbeds, which are subject to flash floods in the rainy season. In Africa they are also known as Babul trees.

Acacias feature heavily in ancient religious tradition and culture. It is written in the Bible that their wood was used to make the Ark of the Covenant. Some scholars believe that the flame-hued flowers of *Loranthus acaciae*, a species common in the Middle East, was the biblical flame that convinced Moses he was standing on holy ground in the presence of God. Although there is no hard evidence to confirm this, it is widely agreed that the wood of the acacia was commonly used during

Biblical times for making all manner of utensils and household items. Its sap, or gum Arabic, was also popular as a medicine for the treatment of inflammation.

Today, acacias grow in abundance throughout the hot climates of the Mediterranean, Mexico and southwestern America, where the cat claw acacia bears thorns resembling those of the angry felines that award the tree is name. Acacia wood is so strong that ship builders in the seafaring heyday of the eighteenth and nineteenth centuries would construct nails from it to hold their hulls together.

Acacia farnesiana, the sweet acacia or needlebush, was brought to Europe in the seventeenth century by Spanish missionaries and planted in the garden of Cardinal Odoardo Farnese (1573-1626), who it was named after. In 1664 the English writer John Evelyn wrote in his *Sylva, or A discourse of Forest Trees and the Propagation of Timber* that 'the French have lately brought in the Virginian Acacia which exceedingly adorns their walks.' Before long, its exotic, intoxicating blossoms were being used in scent-making and to this day *cassie* is a basic note used in a variety of perfumes.

Acacias are also to be found throughout the Australasian continent, where they are called mimosas (or wattles), on account of their foliage which bears a resemblance to the *Mimosa pudica* plant from Barbados, literally 'shy mimic', from the Greek, so named because the leaves shrink when touched. Acacia leaves are actually less sensitive, although they droop at night and in cool conditions. The Albizia, or silk tree as it is known in America, has similar flowers and foliage, introduced to European horticulture by the Italian Filippo degli Albizzi from Africa in 1749.

Early Australian inhabitants made use of acacia trees to build livestock enclosures, naming the trees wattle trees after the woven wattle fences found in Britain. The golden wattle tree, otherwise known as *Acacia pycnantha*, meaning 'densely flowered' is now the floral emblem of Australia. Its beautiful yellow blooms like powder puffs are made up of tufts of sepals. The  bark is used in tanning and the strong wood for building cabins, sheds and houses.

Some acacia species are known to contain certain psychoactive alkaloids, although these are highly variable due to environmental and genetic factors. A substance known as DMT, or dimethyltryptamine, is extracted from the bark and root to induce a psychedelic experience. Mixtures and brews derived from these areas are smoked and drunk and known by various names, including Changa and Ayahuasca.

One species of acacia in particular, Acacia nilotica is said to contain high amounts of DMT and was used long before Amazonian shamans came to use it in their traditional rituals and ceremonies. Although scholars dispute the facts, it is said to have been widely employed by the ancient Egyptians both for its healing qualities and to enhance mystical, religious experiences. So widely revered was this partiuclar species of acacia that it was referred to as the tree of life, symbol of the underworld and of rebirth.

Traditionally acacia was more often used to treat coughs and colds and even gonorrhea and leprosy. Today the sap or gum is said to reduce the risk of heart disease and diabetes. It is a demulcent, relieving irritation in the mouth by creating a protective film and is an ingredient in many cold medications and throat lozenges. It also has anti-bacterial qualities and chewing can control gum disease. Some homeopaths argue that it can even control weight loss.

Acacia tree in the desert near Asluj. *Acacia Tortilis Hayne*.

ALDER

U NLIKE OTHER TREES, a copse of alders, known as a carr (from the Old Norse *kjarr*), can thrive in boggy soil and marshland where there is a poor oxygen supply. Nodules on the roots contain *Frankia alni*, a nitrogen-fixing bacterium similar to those in the legume family, although strictly speaking they are not related. Because of the abundance of Frankia alni red alder delivers vast quantities of nitrogen to the soil beneath and around an alder tree. Red alders can supply up to three hundred pounds of nitrogen per acre and the sitka alder around fifty-five pounds per acre. In many regions this has helped enrich infertile soils. Alders can grow quickly in areas suffering from flooding, fires, landslides and storms.

Alders not only survive where other trees cannot. They possess a striking quality common to all legumes, absorbing metals into their leaves and consequently helping to cleanse the air around them. The catkins visible dangling from an alder branch in autumn and winter are a highly efficient means of reproduction, feather-light so they can be carried on the wind and even float on water.

The blood-like sap of the alder has given rise to many myths and legends. Partly because the tree has the ability to grow in inhospitable places, some of the stories that have arisen are dark and sinister. In Johann Wolfgang von Goethe's *Erlkonig*, or 'Alder King', commonly mistranslated into English as 'Elf king', a boy rides with his father through swampy woodland and hears the Alder King trying to lure him away, but his father hears only the gentle rustling of leaves and sees only the moonlight on the branches and ignores his son's fears. As they arrive at their destination his son is dead.

In other legends beautiful young alder women lure and trap men before transforming themselves into wizened old witches. Such stories were perhaps born because of the alder bark itself, smooth and pale when young, but black and gnarled with age.

The inspiration for this and other dark legends is the *Alnus glutinosa*, which has sticky leaves once used in brooms for cleaning off dust. In old German the tree was known as *elo*, or *elawer*, meaning reddish, the colour of the sap. The common alder is native to the whole of continental Europe and over time species of alder have also been introduced to Canada, Chile, North and South Africa, Australia and New Zealand.

In Asia alders can be found in Turkey, Iran and Kazakhstan and in Africa in Morocco, Algeria and Tunisia. The tree is known as the crucifixion tree, from which, it is said, Christ's cross was made and maybe partly for this reason, although Christ is a Prophet of Islam but not central to the religion, it is not always seen in the Islamic regions of the Middle East.

Alders have also given rise to various other bushy plants. Summersweet or the sweet pepper bush, *Clethra alifolia*, for example, isn't strictly speaking an alder, although *klethra* means alder in Greek and it has leaves like an alder, preferring wetlands, bogs and acid soil. Alder buckthorn, *Frangula alnus*,

is another deciduous shrub related to the alder tree. The genus name *frangula* refers to its brittle wood and both its common name, the alder buckthorn and species name, *alnus,* refer to its association with damp and boggy sites.

For centuries the bark and leaves of the alder have been regarded as having considerable healing properties, providing medicines for various ailments. Research has shown that extracts of the alder's seeds are extremely active against pathogenic bacteria. In his *Travels in North America*, the eighteenth-century plant hunter Peter Kalm wrote 'A Swedish inhabitant of America told me that he had cut his leg to the very bone. He had been advised to boil alder bark and wash the wound often with water and had soon got his leg healed, though it had been very dangerous at first.'

Alder wood has been made into paper and hardboard, for smoking foods, for making clogs and for charcoal. Rich in protein, it tends to be loved by woodworms, so its manufacture for joinery, turnery and carving in ordinary buildings has been releatively limited.

Yet alder's resilience in damp conditions has proved it to be the best possible wood in underwater construction. Today, much of Venice still stands on closely spaced pilings made from the strong trunks of alder trees. The wood came from the westernmost part of what today is Slovenia, resulting in the barren landscapes of the Kras region and from two areas in Croatia, leaving equally desolate slopes in Velebit and south of Montenegro.

Alder tree, *Gerards Herball*, 1633.

ALMOND

A LMONDS WERE EATEN in ancient Greece, where they were
known as *amygdale* and even in the Early Bronze Age
(from around 3000 to 2000BC). Some scholars argue that the
name originated from the Sumerian *amaga*, literally 'great
mother' because in that time and culture the tree was regarded
as sacred. The Romans referred to almonds as Greek nuts. It
was only later that the French called the almond *almande* or
allemande, from which the English name derives.

In Shakespeare's time, as Gerard tells us, Almond trees
were 'in our London gardens and orchards in great plenty.'
There are many references to it in our early poetry. Spenser
alludes to the tree in the *Fairy Queen* 'with blossoms brave
bedecked daintly' and the nuts were widely traded and
consumed during his lifetime.

Almond trees share a common ancestor with peach trees.
Both are classified in the same subgenus category, although
peaches yield edible fruit. The nut is actually the kernel of the
indigestible green fruit born by the almond.

Almond kernels are either sweet (*Prunus amygdalis dulcis*)
or bitter (*Prunus amygdalis amara).* Both varieties contain
almond oil, which has as its major constituent amygdalin, a
naturally occurring compound that when mixed with water or
dissolved in saliva forms prussic acid, or cyanide.

In bitter almonds the amount of amygdalin is much higher,

and has deadly consequences if ingested. In Agatha Christie's Poirot, the scent of almonds is detected in the nostrils of murder victims that have been poisoned. Although bitter almonds should never be eaten, their oil, once separated from the amygdalin, can be used for cosmetics.

Almonds also enjoy a long-standing reputation as a natural healing ingredient. In the Middle Ages almond oil was used to heal skin conditions. Gerard's Herball, later revised and extended by Thomas Johnson in 1633 asserted that almond oil was beneficial in the treatment of urinary conditions on the basis that it 'slackens the passages of the urine and maketh them glib and slipperie... especially if a few scorpions be drowned and steeped therein.' In Christian monasteries monks would mix crushed almonds with water to drink on fast days.

Many religions and cultures old the almond as a symbol of renewal and the almond tree has since antiquity been associated with the idea of hope and rebirth. Trees are native to the Middle East, and throughout Pakistan, Armenia, Azerbaijan, Iran, India and Afghanistan where they are known as *bādām* and herald the arrival of spring. The Bible mentions Aaron's rod, which 'brought forth bud, bloomed blossoms, and yielded almonds'.

In ancient Greek myth Phyllis mourned her beloved Demophon, when he failed to return from war. Upon her death it is said that the gods took pity on her and in their compassion turned her into a tree. Demophon returned soon after, but he was too late. Consumed by his own grief, he fell at the base of the tree, at which the branches burst into sweet blossom. The Greeks believed that this was the very first almond tree, and to this day seemingly lifeless almond twigs placed into warm water will burst into flower.

'Almond tree in blossom', Bethlehem, 1945.

APPLE

THE TREE GROWN in the garden of Eden is perhaps the archetype of all trees. Its fruit even gave rise to the term Adam's apple, when a small piece became lodged in the throat of Adam, the first man, a reminder of humanity's sin.

Indeed, apples appear in many religious traditions, often as a mystical or forbidden fruit. In ancient Greece the apple was sacred to Aphrodite and to throw one was to declare one's love. To catch it was to accept.

The fruit referred to in the Bible, named *tappuach* in the original Hebrew, is not generally grown in the Middle East and were not documented there in ancient times. However, it was maybe the earliest fruit tree to be cultivated. Alexander the Great is believed to have found dwarfed apples in Kazakhstan in 328 BC and those he carried back with him to Macedonia were an important food both in Asia and Europe.

The modern name 'apple' is derived from the Old Icelandic *epli*, and later the Gaelic word, *ubhal* and the domestic British apple tree we know and love today is thought to originate from a mountainous area in the Caucasus. Crab apples or scrab apples as they were known in the past, were common throughout Europe and Asia where they have been consumed for milennia. In ancient Rome Pliny the Elder wrote of the *pomum*, describing different varieties and Pomona, the Roman goddess, was revered as guardian of nature's fruits. As the

Romans invaded Britain, they brought with them the domestic apple, *M.domestica*. Within a short space of time apple trees were widespread in gardens. Christian monasteries had their own orchards and apples were used in cooking and cider-making. Healing balms or *pomatum* were made of apples, rose water and pig fat, and were used as a treatment for hair, giving rise to the term pomade.

Colonists introduced apples to North America, where the first apple orchard was planted by Reverend William Blaxton in 1625. Apple varieties spread along the native American trade routes and were soon cultivated in farms and gardens. By 1845 around 350 varieties were grown in the region and there had been an equal proliferation of apple trees throughout the British Isles. In 1629 the botanist John Parkinson wrote of 'apples so many, and infinite, that I cannot give you the names of all.'

Soon, a few varieties acquired particular popularity, such as the 'Pearmain', so named because it was shaped like a pear, and the 'Costard', shaped like a head, from the medieval slang, *coster*. The Flower of Kent was another favoured variety, said even to have been grown in a garden belonging to the family of scientist Isaac Newton, and although there is no documented evidence of an apple falling upon his head, many still believe that we have the apple to thank for his inspired theory of natural gravity that changed the course of scientific thinking thereafter.

Today, there are over 7500 known cultivars of apple and there are believed to be even more. Worldwide production of apples has reached over eighty million tons annually, with China accounting for almost half of the total yield.

'On the old apple tree'
White rabbits hanging on apple branches during a Winter shoot.

APRICOT

A N APRICOT TREE can belong to several species in the genus Prunus or stone fruits. Usually, an apricot tree is from the species *Prunus armeniaca, meaning* 'plum from Armenia', but the species *P. brigantina, P. mandshurica, P. mume* and *P. sibirica* is closely related. Its varieties have similar fruit and are also called apricots.

Some scholars believe that apricots originated in China, where they were cultivated for their flowers, fruit and kernels and that thanks to the great trade routes between East and West. Apricot trees have been cultivated in Persia since antiquity, and dried apricots were an important commodity. The trees quickly became common throughout the Middle East, Asia and Europe, where they thrived and were known as *al-barquq*, and later in Spain *albaricoque*.

Their introduction to Greece is attributed to Alexander the Great. Later, the Roman General Lucullus (106–57 BC) also would have imported some trees – the cherry, the white heart cherry and the apricot – from Armenia to Rome. Subsequent sources were often confused about the origin of the species. John Claudius Loudon (1838) believed it had a wide native range including Armenia, the Caucasus, the Himalayas, China and Japan. Apricot trees were brought to England during the Middle Ages after Henry VIII ordered the first trees to be procured by his gardener, Wolfe, from Italy. They soon became fashionable. In Latin, apricot means 'precious,' and is also considered one of mythology's 'golden apples'. In England, apricots in dreams were thought to be lucky and were used as an aphrodisiac. In *A Midsummer Night's Dream* Shakespeare's Titania bids her fairies feed her beloved Bottom with 'apricocks and dewberries'. Webster's *Duchess of Malfi* regards them as an inducer of childbirth. However, apricot trees require a temperate climate, with a cool winter to set the fruit but no morning frosts that kill the blossoms, and unsurprisingly they did not flourish here.

In the seventeenth century, English settlers brought the apricot to the English colonies in the New World. Most of modern American production of apricots comes from the seedlings carried to the west coast by Spanish missionaries. Almost all American commercial production is in California, with some in Washington and Utah.

Today, wild apricot trees no longer grow in China, although the Chinese have always associated the apricot with medicine. The classical word 杏壇 (literally: altar) is still widely used in written language. Chuang Tzu, a Chinese philosopher in the fourth century BCE, told a story that Confucius taught his students in a forum surrounded by the wood of apricot trees.

The association with medicine also comes from the common use of apricot kernels as a component in traditional Chinese medicine and from the story of Dong Feng, a physician who required no payment from his patients except that they plant apricot trees in his orchard upon recovering from their illnesses, resulting in a large grove of apricot trees and a steady supply of medicinal ingredients.

In England during the seventeenth century, apricot oil was used against tumors, swellings, and ulcers. Apricot kernels were a key ingredient in traditional healing as early as AD 502. Laetrile, a purported alternative treatment for cancer, is extracted from apricot seeds. It is a myth that apricot kernals contain arsenic. They do not. Apricot kernels do, however, contain cyanide, which is naturally found in many foods common to our diets.

The ingestion of irrational quantities of any of these foods will result in a level of amygdalin the body is unable to safely metabolize. All foods contain substances that are potentially harmful in excessive quantities. and within accordance of the quantities established for safe consumption, they pose no threat. Too much of anything can cause problems. In contrast to the highly toxic treatments being used in conventional medicine, apricot kernels are relatively safe.

The term 'expert of the apricot grove' is still used as a poetic reference to physicians in the Far East and the tree and its fruit enjoys a global reputation as a modern superfood.

A young apricot orchard, Kansas 1931.

ASH

THE EUROPEAN, OR common ash is *Fraxinus excelsior*, literally meaning 'taller' and undoubtedly the tree is easily identified due to its ability to grow to an imposing height. Its roots also penetrate the soil very deeply. In China the ash, known as the Bailashu, or white wax tree, has been cultivated for centuries for the production of a translucent wax coating its feathery leaves, once described as 'the most beautiful, the clearest and whitest that was ever seen'.

Perhaps unsurprisingly therefore, ash trees have been revered throughout time and many cultures have awarded them a sacred status. However, in some European folklore, the ash tree is seen as protective but at the same time malevolent. Anyone who does harm to an ash can find themselves the victim of unpleasant supernatural circumstances.

In Norse legend the tree of life, or Yggdrasil, is depicted as an ash. Its tip reaches as high as heaven, while its roots connect with the underworld and a squirrel climbs its length to connect them. Odin, the great God, is said to have created Ask, the first man, from an ash tree. In Britain ash wood was reputed to repel snakes and the leaves were used to cure snakebites. In 1577, Thomas Hyll wrote snakes were 'mightily displeased and sorest hate the ash-tree.' Hyll was not alone in believing that the tree held healing powers. In the Middle Ages a strange ceremony commonly was performed for the treatment of hernias whereby the trunk of an ash would be cut and the patient – usually a child – would pass through the cleft. Afterwards, the tree would be bound and if the wood subsequently fused the operation was deemed to have been successful.

It was also common practice to make a poultice of ash wood to the legs of cattle and to insert a live shrew into the binding. This, it was thought, would prevent the livestock from straying. Little sympathy was left for the poor shrew.

Myths about the ash's supposed magical powers abounded. If a person was suffering from a fever or toothache, they buried their finger-nail and toe-nail clippings under an ash tree because they believed it would help cure the ailment. Newborn babies in the British Isles were sometimes given a spoonful of ash sap before leaving their mother's bed for the first time. It was believed this would prevent disease and infant mortality. In northern England, it was said that if a maiden placed ash leaves under her pillow, she would have prophetic dreams of her future lover.

But perhaps it is Ireland that holds the richest supply of superstitions regarding the ash. In past centuries and in some parts even today it is said that five trees stand guard over the country and three of these are ash. In rural areas the ash is often found growing near holy wells and sacred springs. It is also believed that crops that grow in the shadow of an ash tree are likely to do less well than those elsewhere.

'The Monmouth Ash', on Shag's Heath, where the Duke of Monmouth, claimant to the throne of England, was apprehended during the Battle of Sedgemoor on 6th July 1685.

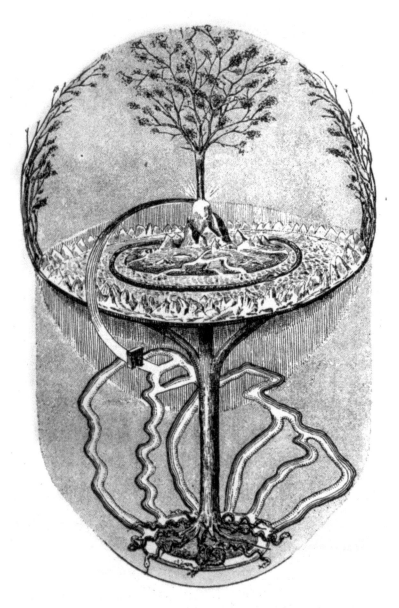

Engraving of the Yggdrasil, the 'Cosmic Ash Tree', nineteenth century.

AVOCADO

T HE AVOCADO IS generally believed to have originated in Mexico, where it has been grown since about 8000 BC, though fossil evidence suggests similar species were much more widespread millions of years ago, occurring as far south as Peru where the Aztec name for the fruit was *ahuacatl* and as far north as California. A water jar shaped like an avocado, dating to AD 900, was discovered in the pre-Incan city of Chan Chan. Its Latin name, *Persea americana,* has led experts in some quarters to believe that it came from Persia (hence Persea), but the name *Persea* more likely originates from the Greek term for another tree, the Egyptian laurel.

Ancient Aztec, Mayan and Inca cultures believed that avocados nourished the body externally as well as internally. To the Mayans the tree was associated with religion, healing, love, mortality, fertility, status and eternal beauty. One account tells how an Indian hero, Seriokai, was able to trace his unfaithful wife to the end of the world. The lovers adored avocados and ate them wherever they went. Seriokai followed the young trees, which sprang from the discarded seeds.he avocado has long been considered an aphrodisiac. Another Aztec legend describes how young and beautiful maidens were kept in their rooms for protection during the height of the avocado season, when consumption of the fruit encouraged illicit behaviour.

Avocados were rather slow to arrive in Europe. The earliest

known account is that of Martín Fernández de Enciso (*circa* 1470–1528) in 1519 in his book, *Suma De Geographia Que Trata De Todas Las Partidas Y Provincias Del Mundo,* but it was 1696 before the first written record in English of the use of the word 'avocado' appeared in Hans Sloane's 1696 index of Jamaican plants.

The following year, in his *A New Voyage Round the World* William Dampier reported that the 'Avogata pear tree' produced a fruit that 'provokes to lust, and therefore is said to be much esteemed by the Spaniards.' Dampier's ship was seized by Dutch slave traders and renamed the *Bachelor's Delight*. There were sixty slave women on board and a healthy supply of avocados.

The avocado tree is unusual in its breeding habits. The tiny flowers are hermaphrodite and open as female on the morning of the first day and close in late morning or early afternoon. Some open as male in the afternoon of the second day, while other varieties open as female on the afternoon of the first day, close in late afternoon and reopen as male the following morning. In order to ensure cross-fertilization trees have to be pollinated from a different tree on the opposite time schedule.

Although notoriously difficult to grow, particularly in Great Britain where a greenhouse or hothouse is required, avocados can prove well worth the effort for their delicious fruit containing many health-giving properties. The creamy pulp is rich in dietary fiber, vitamins and a very good source of mono-unsaturated fatty acids and potassium.

'Picking avocado pears' by John Walter Smith, 1911.

BAMBOO

Under the bamboo
Bamboo bamboo
Under the bamboo tree
Two live as one
One live as two
Two live as three
Under the bam
Under the boo
Under the bamboo tree

So WROTE T.S Elliot in *Sweeny Agonistes,* a telling reminder of the powerful nurturing tree providing shelter and sanctuary that at one time was only to be seen growing in gardens and forests of Asia. Bamboos have always been central in Eastern culture, so much that in China they were named one of the Three Friends of Winter, evergreen and flexible enough to bend without breaking in the fiercest of winds. One classification detailed more than sixty varieties of bamboo during the Chin Dynasty (265 to 420). So integral were they to daily life that they were named one of the Three Friends of Winter, evergreen and flexible enough to bend without breaking in the fiercest of winds. In the third century Chinese poets would refer to themselves as the Sages of the Bamboo Grove. One, named Su Tung-Po, even commented that it would be better to eat 'food without pork than life without bamboo'. Marco Polo described bamboos in his *Travels* as being 'more than three palms in girth and from ten to fifteen paces long', and used in making everything from roofs, mats, baskets and bedding to bows, arrows, sword handles, rope, paper and cooking utensils throughout Asia. Wine, created in Tanzania from species of wine bamboo called *Oxytenanthera braunii*, was widely drunk in the region and still is today. Yet, despite the many and varied uses of the bamboo, some East Asian cultures held that the bamboo should be treated with caution since evil spirits dwelled in its clumps; the denser the clump, the more evil the spirit.

It was the seventeenth century before bamboo was at last brought over to Europe where it was cultivated in greenhouses as an exotic and the nineteenth century before hardy varieties became popular in Western gardens. Derived from the Bambusa genus, nowadays there are 1,400 varieties of bamboo grown throughout the West. They include *B. phyllostachys* (literally' with leaves like corn'), *B dendrocalamus* (meaning 'reed-like tree') and *B. arundinaria* (from the Latin *arundus*, or 'reed'). Some scholars maintain that the common name bamboo is from the Dutch *bamboes*. Others argue that the word bamboo comes from the Kannada term *bambu*, a derivative of the Malian word *mambu*.

Bamboos usually have a life-cycle of around 40 to 80 years, varying among species. Many species blossom infrequently, some at intervals as long as 65 or 120 years. The flowers produce fruit (called 'bamboo rice' in parts of India and China) and the bamboo dies immediately. This is lamentable for all who regard it as a curse or a warning of impending famine; but it is even more so for pandas living in the wild who depend on the succulent leaves and shoots for food and shelter.

'Bamboo shoots' by Hokusai Katsushika, 1760–1849.

BAOBAB

B AOBAB IS THE common name of a genus of trees named *Adansonia*. There are nine species. Six species live in the drier parts of Madagascar, where the baobab is the national tree, two in mainland Africa, and one in Australia. The trees reach heights of 5 to 30 metres (16 to 98 ft) and trunk diameters of 7 to 11 metres (23 to 36 ft).

Few trees can survive the arid heat of the Sahara, but in Africa, where rainfall is scarce, the baobab is in its element. Even in this harsh, inhospitable land it can survive for thousands of years. Unlike many other trees, the baobab has the ability to store up to 120,000 litres of water. Its strong branches, perfectly adept at surviving high temperatures, can sometimes seem more like roots, so much that it is not surprising the Africans call it the upside-down tree.

It is no wonder that the baobab is often referred to as the tree of life. So revered is it that African tribal legend holds that baobab trees originate from heaven and descend upon the earth fully grown and tradition holds that elders meet under the branches of the baobab to take important communal decisions. At Dafkao in Niger there is a baobab so sacred to the Tuareg its trunk is filled with magical signs and symbols in Tifinagh, the Berber script.

Certainly, no part of the baobab is wasted. It provides shelter, food and clothing for the inhabitants of the Savannah. Where water is as precious as gold, the tree is pierced to remove the watery, life-giving liquid within. leaves, seeds and fruit are loved by monkeys and the sweet, fibrous bark is a favourite of hungry elephants.

It was 1592 before the baobab was first documented in European literature, when Prospero Alpini, an Italian plant hunter, described several species of the tree he called *bahobab* in his *Plants of Egypt* and 1757 before another this time French botanist, the extraordinary Michel Adanson, described a baobab 3.8 metres in diameter famed for the carvings made by passing mariners on its mighty trunk.

Two centuries later, in January 1832, Charles Darwin landed from HMS Beagle on St Jago in the Cape Verde Islands and stumbled upon great trees thirty-six feet in girth and also bearing graffiti carvings ' as any in Kensington Gardens'. The ship's surgeon Robert McCormick, who accompanied Darwin, climbed the trunk and carved his initials and the year. The tree is still alive and the initials in tact.

Sadly the same cannot be said for the baobab climbed by Dr Livingstone some twenty years later, when he was travelling by boat between Kalai, an island in the Zambezi, and the Victoria Falls. Although he too observed a 'great burly baobab, each of whose enormous arms would form the trunk of a large tree' and carved his initials, over time others have defaced the trunk with their own messages and obliterated the evidence.

'The Baobab Tree of Kouroundingkoto', taken from the *Illustrated London News*, 1852.

BEECH

OVER THE CENTURIES many people have been unable to resist making their mark on the soft, smooth, silvery bark of beech trees. As the Romans noted, such carvings would only deepen and expand with time and the tree: '*crescunt illae: crescent amores*' – 'as these grow, so does our love,' they said. Evidence of beech bark for writing goes back many centuries and in various cultures. Pieces of bark were used to write upon and were even tied to form the first manuscripts before the advent of mass production of paper.

Despite the elasticity of beech bark, beech wood lacks the strength and durability of other woods because it does not contain tannin. However, it has always been favoured by carpenters in the making of kitchen utensils, as well as in hedges. In the past its leaf buds were also in demand as toothpicks. Beech leaves were gathered to fill mattresses and were considered much more comfortable and longer-lasting than the more universally used straw.

The Latin name used to describe the European beech is *Fagus sylvatica* (literally meaning 'growing in woods'), which is also widely cultivated in North America. The common name 'beech' is of actually Indo-European origin. Their fruit is a small, sharply three–angled nut, borne singly or in pairs in soft-spined husks known as cupules. Beechnuts are edible, though bitter and they carry a high nutrient content. Like acorns they are sometimes known as mast and are often used to fatten pigs in autumn.

Copper beeches were common throughout Europe for centuries, but were not brought to England until the eighteenth century and even then some gardeners disliked them. William Wordsworth was not a fan of the tree, describing one as a blot in his beautiful Vale near Lake Windermere.

Not everyone shared such a dim view of the tree. In cultural history the beech is associated with femininity and is often considered the queen of British trees. In Celtic mythology, Fagus was the god of beech trees. The leaves were used to relieve swellings. Forked beech twigs are also traditionally used for divining.

Nowadays beech timber is used for a variety of purposes, including fuel, furniture, tool handles and sports equipment. The wood burns well and is used to smoke herring. The edible nuts are still sometimes roasted and used as a coffee substitute.

Beech also remains a popular plant for hedging. If clipped it doesn't shed its leaves, and provides a year-round dense screen, which provides an excellent habitat for many birds.

The BEECH TREE Fairy

'In Beech Hill Park', taken from the *Illustrated London News*, 1867.

BIRCH

Give me of your bark, O birch tree!
I a light canoe will build me
Lay aside your cloak, O birch tree!
Lay aside your white-skin wrapper!

And the tree with all its branches
Rustled in the breeze of morning,
Saying, with a sigh of patience,
'Take my cloak, O Hiawatha!

So wrote Henry Wadsorth Longfellow in his 1855 epic poem *The Song of Hiawatha*, in praise of the North American Indians who built heavy-duty, long-lasting canoes out of the bark of the birch tree, sewing the pieces together with its roots. Other cultures made their own use of the lightweight, versatile wood. In Anglo-Saxon Britain light, waterproof 'birce' was used to make shelters and shoes. The buds and leaves were eaten and made beer out of the sap.

On May Day it was customary for children to dance around may poles made of birch trunks and on New Year's Day the old year was swept out with a besom, or a broom, made of birch branches. So strong was the reputation of the birch as a protective, nurturing wood that it was often used to make babies' cradles.

Yet throughout history birch wood enjoyed a mixed

reputation. It is extremely pliable and for this reason it was often favoured in making bundles for whipping those who it was thought needed discipline. The Latin for birch is *betula*, and the Romans carried *fasces*, or birch bundles as a symbol of authority. Thereafter, even loving parents and fair school masters 'birched' young ones as punishment for bad behavior.

In 1551 William Turner wrote in his *New Herball* that it served many good uses 'and for none better than for betynge of stubborn boys, that either lye or will not learn.' Fortunately for children everywhere flexible birch branches also lend themselves perfectly to play, or 'swinging', as the poet Robert Frost called it in his famous early poem, *Birches*. 'One could do worse than be a swinger of birches,' he wrote.

Whatever they are used for, birch trees are undoubtedly beautiful to watch. *Betula pendula*, commonly known as silver birch or warty birch, is widespread in Europe and parts of Asia, though in southern Europe it is only found at higher altitudes. Its range extends into Siberia, China and southwest Asia in the mountains of northern Turkey, the Caucasus and northern Iran.

Silver birches owe their common name to the white peeling bark on the trunk. Indeed, their Sanskrit name *bhrag* means 'shining'. The twigs are slender and pendulous and the leaves roughly triangular with doubly serrate margins and turn yellow in autumn before they fall. The flowers are catkins, light, winged seed widely scattered by the wind. The silver birch is also hardy, a pioneer species, and one of the first trees to appear on bare or fire-swept land. It does not have a long life, only around eighty years, but multiplies effectively through catkins that each contain five and a half million grains of pollen.

The leaves, the twigs, bark and the root are widely used in

traditional medicine; birch is said to have purifying, diuretic, anti-rheumatic and antibacterial qualities. It has been used to dissolve kidney stones and to treat cystitis and other urinary tract infections, as well as cramps and wounds. The salycilates in birch bark have also been used against warts and the bark and buds have been revered for their antibacterial, antiviral and cell regenerative qualities.

Birch was used as paper by scholars and monks since antiquity. The oldest dated birch bark manuscripts are numerous Gandhāran Buddhist texts from approximately the 1st century CE, believed to have originated in Afghanistan. Translations of the texts, mostly in Kharo☐ ☐hī, have produced the earliest known versions of significant Buddhist scriptures, including a *Dhammapada*, a series of discourses that include the *Rhinoceros Sutra*, Avadanas and Abhidharma texts. Sanskrit birch bark manuscripts written with Brahmi script have been dated to the first few centuries. Several ancient Sanskrit writers, such as Kālidāsa, Sushruta and Varāhamihira mention the use of birch bark for manuscripts. The bark of *Betula utilis*, Himalayan birch, is still used today in India and Nepal for writing sacred mantras.

Known in some cultures as the Giving Tree, the birch has undoubtedly played a huge roll in the existence of people and other animals throughout history. In the modern age, the tree is still giving.

'Planting birch tree', Washington, D.C. 1925.

BOX

BOX IS HIGHLY versatile, fast-growing and able to be sculpted, although left to its own devices it will grow into a short, stocky tree with thick, glossy, evergreen foliage. It has been used in hedging and topiary since the Roman age when Pliny the Elder described that growing his own garden as being 'clipped into numerous shapes, some forming letters spelling the garden's name'; and in the formal gardens of sixteenth- and seventeenth-century England box was a familiar sight, usually clipped into elaborate designs, animal shapes or small obelisks.

In the Christian Bible the words of Ezekiel 27:6 literally translated are, 'Thy benches they have made of ivory, the daughter of the ashur tree,' i.e., inlaid with ashur wood. The ashur is the box tree, and accordingly some editions read 'inlaid in box wood'. This is the *Buxus sempervirens* of botanists, noted for the beauty of its evergreen foliage.

Box has not always been to everyone's liking, however. It was seen as a sombre plant and in some areas sprigs of box were given to mourners at funerals to throw onto the coffin. John Gerard, a herbalist writing at the end of the sixteenth century, described box leaves as 'having an evil and loathsome smell', and indeed Queen Anne disliked the smell so much that she ordered any box growing in the formal gardens at Hampton Court and Kensington Palace to be uprooted and discarded.

Due to its high density and resistance to chipping, the wood of the box tree is nevertheless a relatively economical material, and has been used to make a variety of objects since antiquity. The Greeks made small boxes known as *pxides*, from *pyknos* meaning 'dense', referring to the wood itself. To this day the sacred host is kept in a *pyx*. The Romans changed the Greek name to *buxus*, meaning both box and tree.

Once referred to as dudgeon, it has always been used for the handles of daggers. Someone 'in high dudgeon' is indignant and enraged, and while the image of a dagger held high, ready to plunge into an enemy. Macbeth described 'goats of blood on 'thy blad and dudgeon'.

Common box timber is yellow, finely textured and hard. It is used for wood engraving and to make violin pegs and musical instruments. The shrub is commonly used as a topiary and hedging plant in gardens.

In the eighteenth century box was used to make musical instruments, including recorders and woodwind instruments, and was among the traditional woods for Great Highland bagpipes before tastes turned to imported dense tropical woods such as ebony. Still today, a large number of mid- to high-end instruments made are still produced from one or other species of boxwood

Box is not a common tree, however where it is found it can grow in large numbers and it can live for several hundred years. Trees can flourish in many areas, from southern England to northern Morocco, and the Mediterranean region to Turkey. Box thrives on hillsides, in woodland or scrub. A wild population of box is found on Box Hill in Surrey, the North Downs, the Chilterns, Oxfordshire and the Cotswolds.

BREADFRUIT

O N 26TH AUGUST 1768 a small British ship named *The Endeavour* set sail from the English coast towards Tahiti. The primary objective of the expedition, commanded by one Captain James Cook, was to observe the transit of Venus over the sun, but Cook's own journal describes in detail much more and recounts the whys and wherefores of the daily lives of the islanders, including the staple of their diet – the breadfruit.

To the Hawaiians the breadfruit already respresented a god-given gift. Legend held that the breadfruit originated from the sacrifice of the war god Kū. One account tells how, after deciding to live secretly among mortals as a farmer, Kū married and had children. He and his family lived happily until one day a famine seized their island. When he could no longer bear to watch his children suffer, Kū told his wife that he could deliver them from starvation, but to do so he would have to leave them.

Reluctantly she agreed, and at her word, Kū descended into the ground right where he had stood until only the top of his head was visible. Kū's family waited at the place he had last been, day and night, watering it with their tears of concern, until suddenly, a small green shoot appeared where Kū had once stood. Quickly, the shoot grew into a tall and leafy tree that was laden with heavy breadfruits that Kū's family gratefully ate.

Although nowadays breadfruits, or *Artocarpus altilis*, are

widely distributed throughout the Pacific, many hybrids and cultivars are seedless or otherwise biologically incapable of naturally dispersing long distances. People were responsible distribution of the plant throughout the Pacific, from prehistoric groups who colonized the Pacific Islands to those in more recent history.

To investigate the patterns of human migration throughout the Pacific, scientists have used molecular dating of breadfruit hybrids and cultivars in conjunction with anthropological data. Results suggest that Lapita tribespeople are thought to have traveled from Melanesia to numerous Polynesian islands, carrying breadfruit seedlings with them.

Captain Cook wrote at length of the tree that bore this extraordinary fruit. 'It does not indeed shoot up spontaneously,' he wrote, 'but if a man plants ten of them in his lifetime, which he may do in about an hour, he will completely fulfill his duty to his own and future generations.' It was a discovery that at once alerted West Indian colonial administrators and plantation owners seeking cheap, plentiful, high-energy sources of food to feed their slaves in the sugar cane industry.

Among those who saw the potential of the breadfruit was Sir Joseph Banks, who had been accompanying Cook's expedition, was President of The Royal Society. Banks provided a cash bounty and gold medal to encourage exploitation of this rich, natural resource, successfully lobbying his many friends in government and the Admiralty for a British Naval expedition.

It would take almost twenty years before, in 1787, William Bligh was appointed Captain of the HMS *Bounty*, and ordered to proceed to the South Pacific to collect the plants. Banks appointed a gardener for the expedition and gave detailed instructions on how the plants were to be maintained. The *Bounty* remained in Tahiti for five months, during which over eight hundred plants were collected, potted and transferred to the ship, but within a month of leaving many of the crew mutinied, expelling Captain Bligh and supporters in a long-boat, and returned to Tahiti. Bligh survived the ordeal, setting sail with eighteen loyal crew to Timor, which he finally reached in late 1789.

In 1791, Bligh commanded a second expedition with the *Providence* and the *Assistant*, which collected live breadfruit plants in Tahiti and transported these to St Helena, in the Atlantic, and St. Vincent and Jamaica in the West Indies. Although Bligh won the Royal Society medal for his efforts, the introduction was not entirely successful, as most slaves refused to eat the new food, and it was used to feed wild boar and chickens.

Still today, on Puluwat in the Caroline Islands, in the context of sacred *yitang* lore, breadfruit or *poi* is held in such high esteem that it is a figure of speech for knowledge. When studying its strange, hypnotic beauty and many fine qualities, it is easy to see why. Breadfruit is one of the highest-yielding food plants, with a single tree producing up to 200 or more grapefruit-sized fruits per season. It also requires very limited care. Its name is derived from the texture of the moderately ripe fruit when cooked, similar to freshly baked bread; it has a delicious, potato-like flavour. It is not surprising it has become just as worthy a staple to those living in tropical regions who depend upon it.

CACAO

THE ORIGINAL SPECIES of cacao tree from central America is the *criollo*, or native cacao. This small evergreen requires shade and a tropical climate in order to prosper. Its lovely pinkish flowers can sprout directly from the trunk and branches, and are replaced by large pods. To the Azetcs the bitter seeds of the cacao, which we know as cocoa beans were so highly prized that they were used as money and the tree itself was thought to be sacred.

Since antiquity it had been the belief of the Aztecs that *kakaw*, or cacao, had originally been placed by the gods in a mountain, as a gift to humanity. Mayan legend held that a Plumed Serpent gave cacao to the Maya after humans were created from maize by the goddess Xmucane. Thereafter, the Mayans celebrated an annual festival in April, an event that included the sacrifice of a dog with cacao-colored markings, additional animal sacrifices, offerings of cacao, feathers and incense, and an exchange of gifts.

Cacao was offered regularly to a raft of different deities. One important historical document, the Madrid Codex, depicts priests lancing their ear lobes and covering the cacao with blood as a sacrifice. Only men used the cacao beverage in their rituals and drank it before entering into battle and the wood and fruit was believed to be toxic for women and children.

In recent years a team of anthropologists from the

University of Pennsylvania announced the discovery of cacao residue on pottery excavated in Honduras that could date back as far as 1400 B.C. It appears that the sweet pulp of the cacao fruit, which surrounds the beans, was fermented into an alcoholic beverage of the time. Aztec sacrifice victims who felt too melancholy to join in ritual dancing before their death were often given a gourd of chocolate (tinged with the blood of previous victims) to cheer them up.

For several centuries in Latin America, cacao beans were considered valuable enough to use as currency. One bean could be traded for a tamale, while 100 beans could purchase a good turkey hen, according to a sixteenth-century Aztec document.

Christopher Columbus and his crew were the first known Europeans to encounter cacao and chocolate, the products of the cacao tree, when they captured a canoe at Guanaja that contained a quantity of mysterious-looking 'almonds'. Seventeen years later, when the Spanish conqueror Hernando Cortes arrived to meet with Moctezuma in the Aztec capital of Tenochtitlan, he was welcomed and offered chocolate to drink. Cortez and others noted the vast quantities of this beverage the Aztec emperor consumed, and how carefully his attendants prepared it, crushing the beans, mixing them with water and adding powdered chilli peppers, then pouring the mixture from one vessel into another until it became a thick froth. It is said that he was offered the concoction from gold cups served by naked virgins.

Cacao beans, along with other agricultural products, were brought back to Spain, but it seems the beverage made from cacao mixed with sugar to sweeten it was introduced to the Spanish court in 1544 by Mayan nobles and brought from the New World to Spain by Dominican friars to meet Prince Philip. Its popularity grew fast. Spanish ladies were said to drink it in church and on fast days. Priests were known to have a fortifying cup before celebrating mass.

The culinary and medical uses of chocolate soon spread to France, England and elsewhere in Western Europe. By the seventeenth century, the cacao tree was being exploited to produce a fashionable drink, believed to have nutritious, medicinal and even aphrodisiac properties (it's rumored that Casanova was especially fond of the stuff). Samuel Pepys wrote in his diary that he found drinking 'jocolate' 'very good' and it was not long before demand for cacao led the French to establish plantations of cacao trees in the Caribbean, while cacao plantations became common in Spain, Venezuela and the Phillipines.

The fruits of the cacao remained largely a privilege of the rich until the invention of the steam engine made mass production possible in the late 1700s. In 1828, a Dutch chemist found a way to make powdered chocolate by removing about half the natural fat (cacao butter) from chocolate liquor, pulverizing what remained and treating the mixture with alkaline salts to cut the bitter taste. His product became known as 'Dutch cocoa', and led to the creation of solid chocolate.

Chocolate from the cacao tree was always thought to be delicious and good for the health, but in modern times it has become established as a superfood. Experts say that it can improve your memory, increase your bliss, reduce heart disease, shed fat, boost immunity, and create loads of energy. Raw cacao contains nearly four times the antioxidant content of regular processed dark chocolate, twenty times more than blueberries. No wonder the Latin name for the tree, *Theobroma cacao*, means 'food of the gods.'

'Cacao' from an anonymous sixteenth-century engraving.

CEDAR

L ONG BEFORE THE cedar of Lebanon was introduced to European gardens in the late 1700s the tree was already legendary. In ancient Mesopotamia one story told of a battle occurred between the demigods and the humans over the beautiful and divine forest of cedar trees. This forest, once protected by the Sumerian god Enlil, was believed to be completely bared of its trees when humans entered its grounds 4,700 years ago, after winning the battle against the guardians of the forest, the demigods. The account tells that Gilgamesh used cedar wood to build his city.

The cedar famously mentioned so often in the Bible, to whom even God sings praises of honour, is the *cedrus Libani* and as the name suggests originates from the mountains of Lebanon, which were once shaded by thick cedar forests at one time claimed by the Emperor Hadrian as part of his imperial realm. King Solomon also used the aromatic wood of the Lebanese cedar to build the great Temple of Jerusalem, arranging with King Hiran to send 'fourscore thousand hewers' to the mountains to help cut the trees down. The temple beams were massive, strong trunks of ancient cedar trees and the walls lined with heavy cedar planks 'so that no stone could be seen'.

Over the centuries that followed cedar wood continued to be exploited by many other ancient civilisations, including the Phoenicians, Egyptians, Assyrians, Babylonians, Persians,

Romans, Israelites and Turks. Phoenicians used cedars for their merchant fleets and cedar wood made them the first sea-trading nation in the world. The Egyptians used cedar resin for the mummification process and the cedar wood for some of their first hieroglyph bearing rolls of papyrus. The wood was used by native American Indians to make canoes and other boats, as well as weapons, boxes, bowls and baskets and the bark to make blankets, capes and costumes. In modern times, cedar trees are used for making pencils and tools, and during the First World War British troops used cedar to build railroads. However, time, along with the exploitation of the cedar wood, has led to a decrease in the number of cedar trees.

The English name cedar originates from the French term *cèdre*, from the Greek Kedros, but even three hundred years ago it was still rare in Europe. In 1729 Antoine de Jussieu of the Jardin des Plantes in Paris claimed he had smuggled two seedling trees back to France from Lebanon under his hat, watering them with drops from his own drinking supply.

In *The Man who would be King* Rudyard Kipling wrote in praise of the great dense, dark forests of cedars in India and the men 'prickt with palmettoes' whose 'cedar branches raspt their faces', although genuine cedars were still few and far between in his home country of England.

Even today, genuine cedars are usually to be found in Cyprus, North Africa and Asia, although the name has been awarded to other trees such as the red cedar, which is in reality a juniper.

CHERRY

No wonder Alfred Edward Houseman described the cherry tree as the 'loveliest of trees', asserting that his greatest desire was to go about the woodlands 'to see the cherry hung with snow'. The cherry tree has been consumed since ancient times and in many countries. A cultivated cherry is recorded as having been brought from Anatolia to Rome by Lucius Licinius Lucullus in 726 BC. Centuries later a form of cherry was introduced to England at Teynham in Kent by order of Henry VIII who, it is said, tasted and enjoyed eating cherries at Flanders.

The English word 'cherry', French *cerise*, Spanish *cereza* and Turkish *kiraz* all derive from the Greek through the Latin *cerasum*, from the ancient city of Cerasus now known as Giresun in northern Turkey, the place from which cherry trees and their fruit were exported to other parts of the world.

In religious myth the cherry tree has featured equally prominently. Folk songs such as the cherry tree carol reaffirm the cherry's seductive beauty. In it the tree famously bows down allowing Mary, mother or Jesus to pick a bunch of the much favoured fruit; and the cherry featured in many a religious painting as a sign of good fortune.

Cherry trees have been a keystone of oriental cultural life for milennia, prized for their blossom rather than their fruit and planted in imperial gardens where ladies of the royal court would wear pink kimonos echoing the beautiful flowers on the trees around them. The blossom and fruit have always been associated with feminine sensuality and seduction. Poets from East and West alike used metaphors of cherries to suggest far more than a sweet, delicious fruit that grew on the cherry tree.

The beauty of the cherry blossom is a potent symbol equated with the evanescence of human life and epitomizes the transformation of Japanese culture throughout the ages. In America each year, a National Cherry Blossom Festival commemorates the 1912 gift of 3,020 cherry trees from Mayor Yukio Ozaki of Tokyo to the city of Washington, DC. The scions for these trees were taken in December 1910 from the famous collection along the bank of the Arakawa River in Adachi Ward, a suburb of Tokyo, and grafted onto specially selected understock produced in Itami City, Hyogo Prefecture.

The plantings of cherry trees were a unique symbol of friendship to the people of the United States from the people of Japan where the flowering cherry tree, or Sakura, is an exalted flowering plant.

Over the years more and more trees have been given annually and in 2011 approximately 120 propagates from the surviving 1912 trees around the Tidal Basin were collected by horticulturists and sent back to Japan to the Japan Cherry Blossom Association to retain the genetic lineage. Through this cycle of giving, cherry trees continue to fulfill their role as a symbol of friendship.

'A young girl holding a doll remembers the revelry during a festival beneath blossoming cherry trees', Japanese woodcut, *Library of Congress.*

CHESTNUT

CHESTNUTS ARE SOMETIMES referred to as sweet chestnuts and are not the same as horse chestnuts. Sweet chestnuts originated from Persia and evidence dating from 2000 BC records Alexander the Great planting chestnuts on his various military campaigns. But it was the Greeks who named them *castanea* after the Greek city of Kastane and who introduced them to the Mediterranean. A Greek army is said to have survived a retreat in Asia Minor in 401 BC thanks to plentiful stores of chestnuts, on which they depended for sustenance. Ancient Greeks Galen and Dioscordides wrote of its medicinal properties – as well as the flatulence caused by overindulgence.

Chestnut trees are not only widespread throughout Europe, but are common in Asia and America. In Japan, where chestnuts represent success and strength, trees were in cultivation before rice; and China has about 300 cultivars including its native hairy *C.molissina,* recorded three thousand years ago. Often planted in temple gardens and in sacred sites. three species were known: the hairy chestnut, *Castanea mollissima*, the small chestnut, *Castanea seguinii,* and the Henry, *Castanea henryi*. its nuts were said to be the sweetest of any chestnut tree. The hairy chestnut is the most important of the three species, ranging throughout the country. The two other species are still found in the wild state, often mixed in mesic hardwood forests, or in pure stands, especially the small chestnut, found at high elevations in the mountains.

Known by the Romans as *abor panis*, or bread tree, chestnut trees were renowned for their flour, ground from their fruit and used in making a type of bread not dissimilar to polenta. Long before wheat was grown, farmers turned to chestnut bread as a daily staple. Packed with protein and high in nutrients, it was also cheap. In 1583 Charles Estienne and Jean Liebaut wrote of 'an infinity of people who live on nothing but chestnut.'

The popularity of chestnut trees extended widely throughout Britain. Boundary records in the reign of King John already showed the great Tortworth Chestnut in Gloucestershire as a landmark, and it continued its fame under the reign of King Stephen. In his Scottish play, *Macbeth,* Shakespeare wrote of a 'sailor's wife' who had 'chestnuts on her lap'.

Perhaps because chestnut flour did not rise, its popularity was not universal, so much so that in 1664 John Evelyn, writing in his *Sylva,* complained that chestnuts were undervalued and that they were only fed to pigs. In Spain, however, chestnuts continued to thrive and were used to make castanets or *castañas*, literally meaning 'chestnut'.In France the deep colour of the nuts known as *marron* was used to describe hair of a reddish brown and the rich enjoyed delicious sweet *marrons glacées*. The word later gave rise to 'maroon' in English and was used to refer to a type of firework as a result of the sound made by the nuts as they were toasted on the fire.

Charlotte Bronte used the chestnut tree as a metaphor in her novel *Jane Eyre*. The day after Rochester proposes to Jane under 'the great horse-chestnut at the bottom of the orchard,' that same tree gets 'struck by lightning in the night, and half of it split away'. It can't be a good omen to have something that's whole get violently split in half right after two people sitting beside it decide to unite themselves. Much later in the novel

Rochester compares himself to the splintered tree and Jane to a new plant: 'I am no better than the old lightning-struck chestnut-tree in Thornfield orchard...'

In parts of the Indian Subcontinent the sweet chestnut was widely spread during British colonial rule, and particularly common in the lower and middle slopes of the Himalayas. The first settlers in North America discovered the tree growing in its forests, naming it the *C.dentata* on account of its tooth-like leaves and using its strong, durable wood for making new homes.

Chestnuts have a remarkable ability to regenerate from the roots if their stumps are left undisturbed, but sadly they are susceptible to a number of diseases and have encountered several bitter enemies in the twentieth and twenty-first centuries including Ink disease and Phytophthora, a long disease leading inevitably to bark death.

Chestnut blight is a fungal disease that was carried to the West from China, where the native chestnuts had built up a resistance. Despite early legislation intended to halt the import of diseased plants, it was too late. Many great old trees fell victim to the fungus, and although the chinquapin, a smaller blight-resistant hybrid, was cultivated, their fruit is arguably not of the same quality as that of the older American chestnuts.

'Ghost forest of blighted chestnuts', California, 1924.

CHINA FIR

THE CHINA FIR, or *Cunninghamia*, is a magnificent, tall evergreen tree native to China. It has a strong, reddish, heavy trunk and lance-shaped, dark-green leaves.

It is named after Dr James Cuninghame, a British doctor who introduced the species into cultivation in 1702 and botanist Allan Cunningham. James Cuninghame was a Scotsman who travelled to Chusan Island as a surgeon for the East India Company. In 1703 Cuninghame was staying in a village a nearby island and was attacked by Macassan rebels. He was the only survivor. Wounded and imprisoned, he subsequently perished on his return voyage to England.

Many years were to pass before another type of China fir, the *Cunninghamia lanceolata,* literally meaning 'spear-shaped leaves' arrived in Europe, thanks to the Scottish plant hunter Robert Fortune. Fortune, who was famous for introducing tea from China to India, discovered the tree whilst exploring the flora and fauna disguised as a Chinaman and apparently wearing a false pigtail, armed with a large gun, a stick and a Chinese dictionary.

His travels resulted in the introduction to Europe of many beautiful and exotic fruit and plant seedlings, including the cumquat, peony and the azalea, but perhaps it was the Fir that proved to be his most intriguing specimen, receiving mixed reviews in Victorian England. In some quarters the tree became a popular planting for small ornamental gardens, although the celebrated Irish gardener William Robinson hated it, saying that it was the 'most miserable-looking tree... usually full of dead twigs.'

In its native China the wood of the fir has always been valued for its timber, producing a soft, strong, scented wood not unlike the Redwood or the Sugi. In its heartlands of China, Taiwan, north Vietnam and Laos it is used for making temples, bridges, boats, vehicles, furniture and paper.

The Dong, a Kam-Sui ethnic people of the southern territories famed for their sweet *kam* rice, have always regarded the China fir as a sacred tree, a home to spirits who watched over and guarded their settlements. A China fir tree reaches maturity at approximately eighteen years old. In the past it was customary to plant a number of the trees when a child was born. As the trees matured, so did the child and when the child and tree both reached eighteen years, the trees would be felled in order to build a new home for the happy couple.

Traditional belief still holds that benevolent spirits guard the China Fir tree and need to be honoured in order to maintain balance and harmony. For this reason alone, many ancient China firs that might otherwise have died have survived in the region for hundreds of years.

Like many other trees, the China fir is also said to have healing properties. Traditionally the Chinese prized the wood for its medicinal purposes, using it for soothing diseased, fetid feet and in the treatment of poisoning, healing ulcers, cholera and even to alleviate flatulence. Its fragrant essential oil has been used in the treatment of bruises, coughs, rheumatism, burns and wounds.

CHINCHONA

THE CHINCHONA TREE is said to contain such remarkable medicinal properties that the tree inspired the study of homeopathy. It was the Quechua people of Peru, Bolivia and Ecuador, who first discovered its healing properties and who used the bark in the treatment of fevers.

Linnaeus named the tree Chinchona after the Countess of Chinchon, wife of the Spanish Viceroy to Lima. The story goes that the countess was dying from tertian ague, or malaria, when the local villagers persuaded her to bathe in a small pond beneath a Chinchona tree. The pond was bitter due to the quinine in the water, but fortunately the Countess quickly recovered. She was so grateful that she took a supply of the powdered bark home to Spain and distributed among the poor.

Scholars today argue that the account is probably a myth, but it is widely agreed that the bark of the Chincona can and does help in the treatment of malaria. Around the time the Countess fell ill the so-called 'fever tree' bark was introduced into European medicine by Jesuit missionaries, when it became known as Jesuits' bark.

One priest in particular named Jesuit Bernabe Cobo (1582-1657) is credited with taking chinchona bark to Spain, Rome and elsewhere in Italy in 1632. By the 1640s its use was noted in the London Pharmacopoeia. While sales of the bark helped boost the Jesuit order and the Catholic church profited, protestants denied its miraculous healing effects. Oliver Cromwell refused to take what he referred to as the 'powder of the devil' and may have died of malaria as a result.

Charles II took a different view when he contracted malaria. Robert Talbor, his physician, had become famous for his miracle cure and gave the king a dose of the bark in secret – and cured him. Soon after, in 1679, Louis XIV summoned Talbor to Versailles where the doctor cured the young dauphin of the disease. Talbor was rewarded for his success with 3000 gold crowns and a pension for his prescription of seven rose leaves, two ounces of lemon juice and a strong dose of Chinchona bark served with wine, but asked to keep the entire episode secret.

As Europeans ventured further and further into tropical countries and as malaria spread, demand for Chinchona bark stripped supply. The Jesuits recommended planting five trees for every one sacrificed – but it was not enough.

Fortunately, in 1820, two French scientiests, Pierre Joseph Pelletier and Joseph Bienaime successfully isolated the chemical component used in the treatment of malaria and named it *quinguona*.

It was 1865 before Charles Ledger, an English merchant, offered seeds of the Chinchona tree to the Dutch, who successfully established plantations on the island of Java. They bred a new Chinchona, the *C.ledgeriana*, which was easy to grow and rich in medicinal value. Thanks to the Dutch, from then on quinine became cheap and available to all.

Quinine is still used to treat malaria, and can be found in tonic water, although it would be necessary to drink almost twenty litres of gin and tonic daily to achieve the daily dose typically prescribed for malaria.

'Chinchona Nitida Trees', sketch by Mr Pritchett, taken from *A Popular Account of Chinchona Cultivation into British India*, 1880.

CINNAMON

THE CINNAMON TREE is the name given to several species of evergreen native to Bangladesh, Sri Lanka, the Malabar Coast of India and Burma. All are members of the genus Cinnamomum. The botanical name of the tree is Cinnamomum zeylanicum, or 'from Ceylon'. Kinnamom is a Greek word that some scholars say is from 'Kin' meaning China.

Since antiquity cinnamon bark has been peeled from fresh shoots, scraped and dried in the sun to make cinnamon sticks. It was imported to Egypt as early as 2000 BC, but those who report its use often confuse it with cassia. The Egyptians used it for incense, while the Greeks used it to flavor wine. Four types were produced – the bark of *C.verum* from Sri Lanca; *malabathsum*, literally 'dart-tree leaves' from North India; *serihatum* or *C.cassia* from China and the bark of *cinnamomum iners* from Arabia and Ethiopia.

At that time cinnamon was certainly highly valued. Pliny the Elder wrote that a Roman pound of cinnamon cost up to 300 denarii, a huge sum at that time amounting to several months' average wages. Unlike in modern times cinnamon was not used in cooking, but for medicinal purposes and in  embalming. It was said to aid muscle spasms, diarrhea, infections and vomiting. Like other spices, it was also regarded as a powerful aphrodisiac.

Cinnamon is also mentioned in Shennong's legendary 5000-year-old herbal. Shennong was a mythical Chinese emperor and hero of Chinese mythology. His name means 'divine farmer' as, according to popular legend, he taught the people to cultivate many plants. Rumour also credits him with the discovery of the art of tea brewing.

By the third century BC, the Silk Trail, which led from China through Iran and Iraq as far as Tyre, was established, along with the cinnamon industry. Many crusaders, sensing the benefits of trading with the Far East, settled in the ports of Lebanon and Syria and during the twelfth and thirteenth centuries, cinnamon was grown, harvested and traded in the international commercial hub of Venice.

Christopher Columbus hoped to find spices when he sailed to America in 1492 and believed he had discovered the cinnamon tree when he stumbled across the *Canella winterana*, but he was mistaken. It was the late fifteenth century before Portuguese traders discovered the cinnamon tree growing in Sri Lanka and they wasted no time in capitalizing on the bark. In 1636 when the Dutch colonized the island they cultivated cinnamon groves. Heavy fines were levied for possessing an illicit cinnamon stick.

It was the young Carl Linnaeus who classified the cinnamon in 1735 when on a trip through Holland. Carrying only a letter of recommendation, he was invited to visit Dutch the much older botanist Johannes Burman. Burman asked Linnaeus to taste the leaf of the as yet unidentified rare plant he selected and to name it. Linnaeus duly put the leaf into his mouth and at once pronounced it to be a laurel. Burman was impressed. Linnaeus was offered accommodation and employed for six weeks to complete a flora of the plants of Ceylon.

CLOVE

L IKE THE CINNAMON tree, the clove tree is an evergreen. It has large leaves and small scarlet flowers grouped in clusters. The unopened, dried-out buds of these flowers are what we know as cloves.

Clove trees and their aromatic buds have been prized for millennia. Archeologists have discovered cloves in a ceramic vessel in Syria dating back to 1721 BC and there is evidence dating back to the third century BC, which states that a Chinese ruler of the Han Dynasty instructed his audience to chew upon cloves to freshen their breath.

Arab traders carried cloves or *qarumfel* as they were known then along with other traders along the great Silk Routes from east to west and in ancient Greece they were known as *caryophyllum,* or 'nut leaf'. Cloves continued to be traded throughout the Middle Ages and were even offered instead of money. One Muslim writer named Ibn Battuta recounted traders leaving their wares upon the beach and returning to find heaps of cloves as payment.

Traditionally clove trees were native to a few islands in the Moluccas, including Makian, Moti, Tidore and Bacan in the East Indian archipelago and the oldest clove tree is on another island in the group, Ternati. Named Afo, it is thought to be almost four hundred years old. For many years cloves were traded like oil, with an enforced limit on their export, although to the islanders the trees were a symbol of good luck. Clove saplings were traditionally planted for the birth of a new baby.

The Portuguese and subsequently the Dutch established themselves as rulers of the spice islands, eradicating all clove trees except those on the island of Amboine. It is said that a Frenchman named Poivre stole seedlings from these trees in 1770 and sent them back to France and later to Zanzibar. The Dutch monopoly of cloves was thus broken and both Madagascar and Zanzibar became important centres for cloves.

The seventeenth saw a new botanical name for the clove. Traditionally referred to as *Eugenia caryophyllus* after the Greek, now a new genus was named *E.aromatica*, after Prince Eugène, Duke of Savoy. Born in Paris in 1663, the Prince was a soldier who served in Emperor Leopold of Austria's army and owned an estate at Belvedere in Vienna with beautiful gardens that contained a large clove tree. He died in 1736 and the clove *Eugenia* named in his memory. Later, the tree was renamed yet again, this time as a myrtle or Myrtaceae as *Syzgium aromaticum* from the Green syzgos meaning 'joined' on account of the leaf formations.

The medicinal uses of cloves have been long documented in the history of Chinese and Indian Ayurvedic medicine where they have been used as an aphrodisiac for thousands of years. Just as in western herbalism, oil of cloves is still used to help reduce toothache. Clove contains significant amounts of an active component called eugenol, which has made it the subject of numerous health studies, including studies on the prevention of toxicity from environmental pollutants. Nowadays they are used homeopathically to treat acute flares of autoimmune diseases and are traditionally used to treat stomach and digestive problems, noted for their ability to fortify the kidney, calm morning sickness and diarrhea and even to treat hiccups.

Today the buds of the clove tree are frequently used in

African, Asian and Middle Eastern cooking in both sweet and savoury dishes. In Mexican cuisine they are known as *clavos de olor*, and often combine other spices such as cumin and cinnamon to add flavour and aroma to a dish. In Great Britain no glass of mulled wine would be without them.

The world's oldest living clove tree is called Afo, although no one knows how exactly it aquired that name. Neither is it exactly certain when Afo was planted, although rough estimates suggest it is between 350 and 400 years old. Standing at nearly 40 metres tall and over 4 metres round, it towers upon the slopes of the volcano Gamalama on the spice island of Ternate. Afo was planted in defiance of the Dutch ban nearly four centuries ago. Above all, this ancient, massive clove tree remains a symbol of the ultimate folly of man and the stubborn refusal of nature to be controlled.

Zanzibar. Motor road bordered by clove trees and stately palms.

COCONUT

Technically speaking, the coconut palm or *Cocos nucifera* is actually a stemmed plant, although we think of it as a tree and it is known as one. It has no bark and is more like a grass. It is a member of the palm family, or *Arecaceae* and the only accepted species in the genus *Cocos*.

Coconut trees thrive in hot sandy soil by spreading their dense shallow roots over great distances. Unlike many other trees they do not have a tap root and are highly tolerant of salt, although for optimum growth they require high humidity. On beaches their bendy trunks can withstand strong sea winds. As the tree grows upwards, the lower leaves and branches drop off, giving them their characteristic crown shapes, as if they are stretching heavenwards. Coconuts are generally grouped into two types: tall and dwarf. Both produce their first fruit in six to ten years and take between fifteen and twenty years to reach peak production. On fertile soil a tall palm can yield around seventy-five fruits a year, but often the crop is far less.

Scholars have debated the origin of the coconut tree for decades. Some argue that the tree originated in South-east Asia and that spread around the world by riding ocean currents, but explorers such as Christopher Columbus did not record seeing them when they sailed to America or the West Indies. Evidence exists showing fossils of the coconut dating from as far back as 55 million years ago in Australia and, although they were unknown in ancient Rome and Greece, they were known to be widespread on the Pacific Coast at that time and some scholars believe that they came to Egypt courtesy of Arab traders in the sixth century. When Marco Polo discovered coconuts at the end of the thirteenth century he called them Pharoah's nuts.

Spanish explorers brought coconuts to South America, but it was not until the end of the nineteenth century that a ship named the Providencia brought coconuts to America. It was carrying a large cargo of coconuts from Havana to Barcelona when on 9th January 1878 when it was wrecked off the coast of Florida. Coconuts were washed ashore and began to flourish there. From then on, the land was known as Palm Beach.

The term coconut is derived from sixteenth century Portuguese and Spanish word *coco*, literally meaning 'head' or 'skull', from the three indentations on the shell that resemble two small eyes and a mouth, although some argue that it is derived from the slang word meaning 'grinning face' are actually scars where the coconut was attached to its stem before it fell to the ground and enable a new shoot to grow through. It is an urban myth of modern times that more deaths are caused by falling coconuts than by sharks.

Those living in the tropics have their own legends that tell how the coconut was named. One, originating from the Phillipines recounts how a long time ago, a Chamorro family that was part of the Achote tribe, had a young daughter and she was very beautiful, for this reason she had many admirers. One day the young girl was very thirsty and she asked people for the juice of a special fruit, everyone tried to find the fruit to give to the young girl, but they couldn't find it. Sadly the girl got sick for the thirst and died.

The father took the girl's body and buried it on a hill near the village. Then he put a beautiful headstone, which was covered with flowers by the people. One day, the villagers saw that a plant they never saw before started to grow on the girl's grave, they built a shelter to protect the tree. After some years passed by, the plant grew twenty feet tall. The tree had a strange fruit that grew in it and one of them felt to the floor and cracked open. The chief called the father of the girl to eat the fruit, but he refused, calling the girl's mother to eat it. She described the fruit as chewy and sweet From that day on, the plant was called coconut tree.

Coconuts are technically drupes or stone fruits, rather than nuts. They are so impenetrable they can float on the sea without losing their ability to germinate. It is often said that coconuts can travel for 110 days or 3,000 miles and still be able to germinate. It takes about a year for a nut to mature and the young nuts are full of liquid, which gradually turns solid.

Today coconut trees are grown in ninety countries and produce 62 million tons of coconuts. They are common throughout the Middle East, Sri Lanka, the United States, Northern Australia, Bermuda, India, Indonesia and the Philippines. Although they are grown in the tropics for decoration, virtually every part of the coconut tree is made use of by man and has significant value. In Sanskrit it is *kalpa vriksha*, or 'the tree that provides all the necessities of life'. In Malay it is *pokok seribu guna*, 'the tree of a thousand uses'. It is the national tree of the Maldives and considered so important there it is the national emblem.

Coconuts are used in many ways. The sap of the tree can be drunk. Milk, made from pressing the meat, is also an everyday ingredient in Eastern and Middle Eastern cooking, as well as being used in industry, detergents and even plastics. The fibrous husks, known as coir, are employed in rope-making, brushes, sacks, caulking for boats, mattress stuffing and mats and the shells are used for fuel and as a source of charcoal. Coconut oil, made from pressing dried coconut meat, is used widely in cosmetics, skin creams and cooking and the fronds are used in broom-making. Wood from the coconut trunk is used for building small bridges and huts and, in Hawaii, for making canoes. No wonder those living in the Philippines call it the tree of life.

Zanzibar. Pile of coconuts in a grove.

COFFEE

THE COFFEE TREE is a member of the Rubiaceae family and is native to tropical regions of Africa and Asia. It provides one of the most economically valuable and widely traded crops in the modern world. Several species of coffee tree are grown today, although the *coffea Arabica* accounts for almost eighty percent of the world's coffee production. This variety, as with all coffee trees, produces edible red fruits or 'cherries', each containing two seeds or coffee beans.

Coffea Arabica is notoriously difficult to cultivate. Able to withstand low temperatures, it is not hardy to frost and is vulnerable both when grown in poor PH soil, as well as being susceptible to a variety of pests. For these reasons it is still mainly cultivated and harvested in its native Brazil, Java, Indonesia, Sumatra, central America and East Africa, and also assorted islands in the Caribbean and the Pacific.

According to Ethiopian popular legend, *coffea Arabica* was first discovered to produce coffee after goats were seen mounting each other after eating the leaves and fruits of the coffee tree. One popular story dating from the first century tells of a goatherd called Kaldi. It was said that Kaldi, a Christian, tasted the berries and took them to a nearby monastery, upon which one of the resident abbots, regarding them as too bitter, cast them onto the fire. The aroma of roasting coffee beans kept the abbot and his fellow monks alert on their night vigils thereafter.

The first written record of a drink being made from the roasted beans of the coffee tree originates from Arab scholars writing in the eleventh and twelfth centuries. By then it was commonplace in Egypt and Turkey. Cultivation of the tree in Yemen is also well documented at this time, where by the fifteenth century a drink made from the fruit of the coffee tree was drunk widely in Sufi monasteries.

It was the sixteenth century before the popularity of coffee extended to the West, when the bean was introduced to the island of Malta through slavery. Seedlings were smuggled on sailing ships by botanists captivated by the exotic plant that was seen to hold vast commercial potential. In 1573 the German plant hunter Leonard Rauwolf described a drink known as 'chaube' derived from the tree that made him feel animated and which was expertly brewed by Muslim Turks, despite its intoxicating effect. Within several decades coffee was being drunk widely throughout northern and southern Europe. Traded between Venice, North Africa and the East, coffee beans were shipped to Britain, where coffee houses became swiftly established. In London men would gather to drink coffee and discuss politics. Not everyone approved. Even at this time, some argued that coffee had a detrimental effect on the health. Carl Linneaus, himself a coffee drinker, wrote of several deaths of those who had overindulged.

Whatever objections there were to the fruits of the coffee tree, its popularity was irreversible and plantations became widespread, often on the back of slave labour. Despite the hardships endured by those working to raise crops, generations of coffee fans followed. Honoré de Balzac put his creative inspiration down to the half a dozen cups he drank a day a day. Ludwig Beethoven made his coffee using sixty beans a cup.

'Arbre du café dessiné en Arabie sur le naturel', *Library of Congress*, 1846.

CORK

THE CORK TREE, *Quercus suber*, is an evergreen oak that grows naturally in North Africa, France, Italy, Spain and Portugal. Cork oaks live to about three hundred years and their thick, strong bark can be harvested to produce cork, a unique natural material that is both lightweight, highly flexible and watertight. No wonder it has so many commercial uses, from wine stoppers to sandals, soundproofing, flooring, fishing floats and buoys to badminton shuttlecocks.

Taking cork from the tree does not harm the tree. Within a short space of time the bark simply regrows producing a new layer of cork. Cork is the outer bark of the tree and is made up of dead cells, the gaps between which are air-filled. These qualities have ensured that the bark of the cork has been in great demand for centuries. In 1654 John Evelyn wrote of Grecian ladies wearing cork sandals, describing how lightly and prettily they trod.

One legend originating in Bologna from the time tells how in a chapel a statue of the Virgin Mary had become tarnished. A local shepherd, seeking to care for it, took it away and placed it into the trunk of a cork tree. He visited every day, playing his flute and singing to it. But the poor, well-meaning shepherd was had for stealing and condemned to death. Fortunately, it is said, the Virgin Mary herself stepped in, returning the statue and the shepherd to their rightful places by the tree. The local villagers, seeing what they believed to be a miracle, honoured the tree and the shepherd received a pardon.

In 1813 Thomas Jefferson planted cork acorns in America, although without significant success, but today two million hectares of cork forest are grown for harvesting worldwide, much of it in Spain and Portugal, producing about 200,000 tons of cork. Synthetic materials have replaced natural cork in some areas, but cork continues to be prized and admired due to its natural sustainable nature.

Phellodendron amurense, the bark of the Amur cork tree, has been used in ancient Chinese medicine for thousands of years and has a long history of healing powers. Throughout Chinese history, it has been used as one of the fifty fundamental herbs, typically administered as a painkiller.

Researchers at the University of Texas Health Science Centre have recently discovered that cork tree extract can help prevent the scarring that blocks anti-cancer drugs from entering and killing cancer. *Phellodendron amurense* prevents fibrosis from occurring around the tumour gland and has been found to suppress an enzyme which causes further inflammation within the tumours.

Perhaps the ancient Chinese remedy could eventually be integrated into cancer treatment. As a first step, the extract has now been made available as a dietary supplement and has been deemed safe for use by cancer patients.

'Cork harvesting in the New World', illustration by Joshua Davies, 1911.

CYPRESS

THE NAME CYPRESS is derived from the old French *cipres* and in turn from the Latin *cypressus* and Greek *kuparissos*. Kuparissos was a youth who lived in Cea and who was said to be beloved of the Greek Gods Apollo and Zephyrus. The story goes that Apollo once gave Kuparissos a stag as a gift, which the lad accidentally killed. Filled with remorse, Kuparissos would not forgive himself. So, legend has it, Apollo turned him into a cypress tree.

Although the cypress tree is an evergreen tree and in this symbolizes hope, the story of Kuparissos an extremely sad and dark one. Perhaps it is unsurprising that it is often found in cemeteries and associated with mourning. Even in ancient Egypt the Cupressus tree was used in the making of sarcophagi. In Classical times it came to be associated not just with Apollo, but with Hecate, a goddess of the underworld and Athenian households grieving for lost loved ones were often garlanded with cypress branches. The tree itself is also unable to regenerate, unlike some other trees.

Cypress trees are nevertheless to be found in many countries today. The island of Cyprus is named after the tree and it is impossible to imagine Italy without its cypresses. In France Vincent van Gogh painted their thick, swaying branches at San Remy shortly before his death; and there have been cypresses alternating with fruit trees for centuries throughout Spain and

Portugal. They are equally popular in the Middle East, starring in Muslim gardens from Turkey to Iran. In one Persian garden stands a cypress thought to be the oldest on earth. Named the Sarv-e Abarkooh, it is to be found in the province of Yazd and thought to have stood there for around four thousand years.

Nowadays, not all trees referred to as cypresses are in fact cypresses, however. Many conifers are similar in appearance and there are also many different species. This confusing situation has given rise to a number of falsely named cypresses and hybrid varieties. The *C.lawsonia* is a prime example of one such variety. First sent to Scotland in 1855 by William Murray to his colleague Charles Lawson, Murray's seeds grew into trees that from that time on flourished in British gardens.

False cypresses are by no means confined to Britain. The Mexican cypress, known as the cedar of Goa, is another example of a species that is referred to as a cypress, but which is not really one. It is similar to the Monterey cypress, or *C.macrocarpa*, named by Karl Theodore Hartweg in 1846 because of its close resemblance to the cedar of Lebanon.

In North-western America another false cypress is common. The *C.nootkatensis*, or 'stinking cypress' is known for its unpleasant-smelling leaves. And in the Middle East and South America the *C.sempivirens* and the *Fitzroya cupressoides* named after Captain Fitzroy of the Beagle can both live up to a thousand years, but they are still not true cypresses.

Wherever they have populated the soil, cypresses have been exploited in traditional medicine. Some believe that the bark can treat ovarian dysfunction and to relieve the symptoms of the menopause. Cypress oil, distilled from the leaves and branches, is used in many perfumes and aftershaves.

'Reproduction of illustration showing a dragon, cypress, and blossoming tree', *Library of Congress*, 1857.

DATE PALM

R ESPECT DATE PALMS, which are your relatives. Because the first date tree was created with the same mud from which Adam was created.' So said the Prophet Muhammad, whose favourite food, along with watermelons, was fresh dates. Indeed the date palm and its fruit are considered so blessed under Islam that it is said that Maryam, or Mary, gave birth to Jesus under a date palm and that the tree offered her its fruit.

Dates have always been a benchmark throughout the Middle East where the climate is perfect for them. The trees require moisture beneath the root system, but the top leaves must remain dry. Dates are wind pollinated and are either male or female. Natural pollination occurs where there are an equal number of male and female trees, but with assistance one male can pollinate up to 100 females. The trunk is not a bark in the same sense as many trees. It grows upward rather than outward. There are also no branches, but a crown of leaves that it is said stretch heavenwards.

Fossil evidence exists showing that the date palm has existed for fifty million years and in the Middle Eastern desert from at least 6000 BC. The tree is believed to have been cultivated in the Indus Valley, Mesopotamia and ancient Egypt from as early as 4000 BC. Romans and Greeks used the fruit to make date wine. Date palm seeds have an extraordinary capacity to survive, sometimes for thousands of years. Several archeologists have succeeded in successfully growing seeds discovered on historic sites. In 2012, scientists in Russia were able to grow a plant from 32,000-year-old seeds that had been buried by an Ice Age squirrel in Siberia. And a male date palm tree named Methuselah that sprouted from a 2,000-year-old seed nearly a decade ago is thriving today, according to the Israeli researcher who is cultivating the historic plant. The plant was sprouted in a laboratory in 2005, grown from ancient seeds recovered at archaeological sites around the Dead Sea

Arabs transported dates to Europe where they continued to be enjoyed by royalty. Then as now every part of the tree is used. The leaves are employed to make bedding and roofing and the fibres are used in weaving baskets and for ropes.

Date palms trees do not particularly favour the colder climes of the northern regions. In the eighteenth century Karl Linnaeus named the tree *Phoenix dactylifera*, literally 'finger' in his *Systeme Naturae*. The analogy is an apt one, referring to the date fruits that are shaped like long human digits and which hang from the tree in great pendulous bunches. 'Pheonix' refers to the mythical bird that died and rose again from the ashes of a fire, suggesting the tree's ability to withstand high temperatures and its symbolic reputation as the tree of life, death and rebirth in many cultures.

'Date palms in Karnak, Egypt, 1911', *Library of Congress*.

EBONY

S HAKESPEARE WROTE 'A wife of such wood were felicity,' of the ebony, and it is easy to see why. The wood of the ebony tree is so fine and smooth when polished that it continues to be one of the most luxurious and expensive in the world. So dense and hard is ebony that no nail can be driven into it and it is so heavy that it sinks when placed in water.

These unique qualities have ensured that it has always had many uses, employed in the making of piano keys, clarinets and plectrums. By the end of the sixteenth century fine furniture was being made of the wood in Antwerp. Carvings and refined mouldings were crafted for the aristocracy and cabinets were made in Paris by skilled craftsmen who became known as *ébénistes*. Today, everything from cruxifixes, black pieces in chess sets and handgun grips to the butts of pool cues can be hued from the wood.

The name ebony, literally meaning 'food of God', is derived from the ancient Egyptian *hbnu* and indeed pieces of it have been uncovered from many Egyptian tombs where they were offerings. Pluto, king of the underworld was said to have had a throne made of ebony, and the Ephesians held the wood and tree in high esteem, believing that they were a direct gift from the gods, a token of strength and beauty. Perhaps because of the deep, rich black colour of the wood, unsurprisingly ebony was once associated with death. It was even believed to be poisonous. In the fourteenth century Sir John Maundeville wrote during his travels in the East that there was a certain table of ebony, or black wood, 'that once used to turn into flesh on certain occasions, but whence now drips only oil, which is kept above a year becomes good flesh and bone.' Hamlet's ghost claimed to have been murdered with cursed 'Hebanon' poured into his ear, and many scholars believe this to refer to ebony.

Different species of ebony are native to southern India and Sri Lanka (*Diospyros crassiflora*) and Indonesia (*Diospyros celebica*), as well as Mauritius (*Diospyros tesselaria*), where trees can grow up to seventy feet. The Latin name *diospyros* means 'divine fruit,' and ebony fruits are sweet and succulent. They range from lemon to apple-sized and are attractive looking, making them ideal for large-scale marketing. The fruits are commonly eaten fresh, dried, or pulped for sauces. They can be used in porridges and toffee, brewed into beer, fermented into wine, and distilled into an ebony brandy. In Namibia they are made into a hot liqueur called *ombike*. The bark of some ebony species is boiled to make a dark blue dye for cloth. The injured bark of a live tree secretes a gum that is useful as a glue. The roots of the jackalberry tree are made into a mixture for treating dysentery and fever. The mixture has also been used to help treat leprosy in Southern Africa.

Ebony wood is now extremely rare and these days many species are so depleted that ebony is considered to be under threat and in Sri Lanka ebony is a protected tree. Africa suffers badly from illegal felling. Buying and selling the wood is punishable by imprisonment, yet it has done little to deflate the large, international underground trade.

ELDER

OVER TIME MANY myths, often conflicting, have sprung up regarding the elder tree. Even though the elder is a small tree and not widely known in the Middle East, it was once believed that Judas Iscariot hanged himself from an elder tree. A fungus that grows on elders that is shaped a little like a human ear was known as *Auricularia Judae*, or 'ear of Judas'. And in Scotland, where the elder is known as the 'bour-tree', an old rhyme points to the tree's small stature and crooked branches as punishment for its part in Jesus' death: 'Bour-tree, bour-tree, crookit rung, never straight and never strong, e'er bush, and never tree, since our Lord was nailed t'ye'. Unsurpisingly the maligned tree soon became synonymous with the devil himself. Many feared to burn elder-logs for fear they would 'bring the devil into the house'.

Other folklore tells of mixed magic, both black and white, and a female sheltering presence. One legend holds that if an elder was cut down, the Elder Mother would be released and take her revenge. This belief is also found in Eastern England. In Lincolnshire until quite recently, it was important to ask permission of the 'Old Lady' or 'Old Girl'. The correct way to approach the tree was to say: 'Old Woman, give me some of thy wood and I will give thee some of mine when I grow into a tree'. If this procedure was not adopted, ill-luck could befall. The Elder-Mother, who may well once have been a powerful female figure venerated for the healing properties of her tree, became feared as a witch in Medieval times. In Ireland, witches were thought to use elder boughs as magic horses, while in England the crooked-branched tree was thought to be the form of a bent old witch, who would bleed if she were cut.

In other regions the elder tree was said to actively ward off witches and give protection. A sprig of elder was put into a coffin as protection against evil and the driver of a horse-drawn hearse would carry a whip made of elder to ward off bad spirits.

However mixed its reputation, the elder has been used for centuries in the treatment of disease. In 1664 John Evelyn wrote that the elder was a 'catholicum against all infirmities'. Water steeped in elderflower was widely used for inflammation throughout the Middle ages and elderberry wine as a mood booster. Elderflower bark was strained and drunk by many suffering from colic, believed to be beneficial to digestion, to relieve allergies, heal coughs and colds and generally boost respiratory health. In Chinese medicine it was used to treat rheumatism and traumatic injury.

Resonant and finely grained, the wood of the elder has always been used in making a variety of musical instruments, especially flutes and other wind instruments. Pliny wrote that shepherds would cut a horn or trumpet from the wood of an elder to summon their flocks. Later on, the branches of elders were a favourite in hedgemaking.

Elder trees flourish without propagation and nowadays many species of the elder, or Sambucus, can be seen throughout Europe, parts of Australasia and South America. They are grown for their blossom and fine foliage and are loved by humans and butterflies alike.

ELM

WHEN ALFRED, LORD Tennyson, wrote of a place of 'immorial elms' where 'doves moaned' he was describing a perfect, drowsy summer's day in the English countryside. Elms do prefer to grow in lush, green regions and until recent years great elm trees could be spotted throughout Great Britain, as well as fertile lands elsewhere in Europe.

In the late twentieth century Dutch elm disease has devastated elms wherever they lie. Named on account of the Dutch botanists Bea Schwarz and Christina Johanna Buisman who first described it, the disease is caused by a small beetle called Scolytus. As the eggs of the female hatch, they carry a fungus to the tree as they feed and the tree, because it does not have an immune system, is powerless.

It is by no means the first time that the elm has fallen foul to disease. Somehow the tree has won through. This vulnerable tree was already under attack in ancient times. So many trees died in 4000 BC that the elm decline is still used by scientists to date prehistoric pollen deposits.

Many centuries later in January 1862 a new spate of disease was reported in the London Times, at which point it was believed elms were on the brink of extinction. The elm responded with strength. It won through once again.

Elm timber has been used for making bows, hubs of wheels, coffins and Japanese drums for centuries and its fibres have been exploited in rope-making. In Classical times elm provided wood for making vine supports. Ovid described the elm as *ulmus amat vitem, vitis non desertit ulmum.* In the Middle Ages elm wood became prized for its interlocking grain and consequently its resistance to splitting.'Wych', as it was known then, meaning 'bendable' or 'pliant', was even eaten. The seeds are high in protein and nutrients and boiled elm bark sustained much of the rural population of Norway during the great famine of 1812.

In Scotland wych is the more common species. and in Gaelic it is known as 'leven', as in Loch Leven in Kinross, and was valued for its roles in the dyeing of wool. Intermittent colours in woollen yarns could be introduced by way of an early form of tie-dyeing. Twine made from the inner bark of the elm tied tightly at regular intervals, to form 'hanks' of the yarn, was used to stop a dye from reaching the wool. A yellow dye could also be derived from the elm, and the leaves were fed to livestock when other fodder was scarce.

Elm trees have also enjoyed a rich folklore. In Greek myth Orpheus, having rescued his wife Eurydice from the underworld by enchanting everyone there with his harp music, paused to play her a love song, at which spot the first elm grove was said to have sprung up. For the Celts elm trees were also associated with the underworld. The trees had a special affinity with elves who were said to guard the burial mounds, their dead and the associated passage into the afterlife.

Conservationists working in the twenty-first century continue to strive to protect the elm, a beautiful tree once depicted by artists from Frederick Chide to John Constable.

'Washington elm', from *Picturesque America*, edited by W.C. Bryant, 1894.

EUCALYPTUS

THERE ARE ALMOST seven hundred species of eucalyptus. Almost all are to be found in Australia where they are known as gum trees on account of their large quantities of sap. Almost all species are evergreen and intolerant of frost. Yet ancient evidence of eucalyptus trees originates not from Australia, but from South America where fossils have been discovered dating back to the early Eocene period almost twenty one million years ago.

In Australia, the eucalyptus has been the tree of folklore where children sing of the 'kookaburra in the gum tree.' Aborigines have enjoyed the sweet flakes of the manna gum for centuries, using medicine found in its oils which has been used to cure everything from an upset stomach to a nasty laceration. The eucalyptus provided the early Australian settler materials for buildings, implements, and desperately-needed fuel. Its versatility was virtually unchallenged by anything else on the Australian continent.

The first European to describe eucalyptus was the botanist William Dampier, who in 1688 wrote of the 'gummy substance' oozing from them. In 1770 another botanist, Joseph Banks, accompanied Captain Cook on the *Endeavour*. Banks wrote of the tree and collected specimens of *E.gummifera*.

Later, in 1777 on Cook's third expedition, David Nelson collected a tree on Bruny Island in southern Tasmania and carried it home to the British Museum in London and only now did it acquire its name. *Eucalyptus obliqua* was so called by the French man L'Heritier, who coined the name from the Greek 'eu' and 'calyptos, literally 'well' and 'covered', on account of the operculum of the flower buds. From then on the trees were introduced to many countries, notably Brazil, Ecuador, Morocco, Portugal and Spain, South Africa, Israel and Chile.

As with other members of the myrtle family, eucalyptus trees have leaves covered with oil glands. The oil is highly flammable and bush fires spread fast through the oil-laden air of the tree canopies and also because of the leaf litter on the ground beneath. Trees caught in forest fires have even been known to explode.

But the aromatic oil from the eucalyptus is also a blessing. Popular in the treatment of all manner of ailments, at one time it was even thought to cure malaria. Today the oil is in demand. An efficient antiseptic, it is used widely in toothpaste, cough pastilles and degongestants. It is also an active ingredient in mosquito repellants.

Eucalyptus is associated with good luck and prosperity, especially when it concerns knowledge. For instance, using eucalyptus in a ritual seeking a positive result to pending news is said to be beneficial. Worn as a charm, this wood is believed to promote positive luck for the wearer. It is also an excellent tool in divination and used to make didgeridoos after termites hollow the branch. Above all, the leaves are essential to koala bears who feed almost exclusively on them and depend on them for their survival.

'Eucalyptus tree grove, 1900', *The British Library.*

FIG

THERE ARE ABOUT 850 species of fig tree, or *Ficus*. The common fig, *Ficus caria*, is native to the Middle East and Western Asia, where it has been cultivated since ancient times. Indeed, nine fossil figs dating back to 9400 BC were discovered in the Jordan Valley in a crop that predates wheat, barley and even vegetables.

Figs were a common food in ancient Rome. Pliny described them in the first century AD and Plato documented that Greek athletes at Olympia were fed diets of figs to increase their running speed and overall strength. Cato wrote of several fig varieties during his lifetime and presented a handful of fresh figs to the Senate. By doing so, he was accusing those present of weakness and effeminacy.

In Greek mythology Apollo was thirsty and sent a crow to collect water from a stream. However the crow, chancing upon a fig tree, waited for the fruit to ripen. Knowing his was late and would be chastised, the crow took back a snake along with the water he had collected. His plan was to blame his delay on the snake. But Apollo saw through the crow and cast bird, goblet and snake into the sky where they became star clusters.

Figs feature equally prominently in various religions. The Jewish King, Hezekiah, was cured of a life-threatening plague by applying figs to the infected spot. Fig trees and their fruit also figure widely in the Bible. It is written that Jesus, passing a fig tree bearing no fruit was so displeased he cursed the tree. From then on the branches drooped and the tree withered.

In Buddhism the fig tree features equally prominently. Buddha achieved enlightenment under an old, sacred fig known as a *Bodhi*. In the Islamic sayings of the Prophet, Muhammad is reported to have said 'If I had to mention a fruit that descended from paradise, I would say this is it because the paradisiacal fruits do not have pits. Eat from these fruits, for they prevent hemorrhoids, piles and help gout.

Hindu mystics have for centuries meditated beneath sacred fig trees and have practised *pradakshina* (circumambulation, or meditative pacing) around the sacred fig tree as a mark of worship. Usually seven *pradakshinas* are made around the tree in the morning time chanting *vriksha rajaya namah*, meaning 'salutation to the king of trees.' Hindus believe that twenty-seven constellations represent twelve houses, or *rasis*, and nine planets. All are specifically represented precisely by trees, one for each star. The fig symbolises Pushya.

Figs were transported to North America by Spanish missionaries in 1769 and the Mission variety is still widely cultivated there. Figs prospered in the warmer climes of southern Europe. Today, Turkey is the chief cultivator of commercial fig trees, producing twenty-seven per cent of the world's annual one million tons of fruit. Nowadays figs are eaten fresh as well as dried and are used in jam-making. They are a source of fibre, and a rich source of vitamins, manganese and phytochemicals.

'Fig tree', watercolour by William Berryman, 1808.

FIR

THERE ARE AROUND fifty species of fir in the family *Pinacae*. They are to be found growing abundantly throughout Europe, Asia, Northern Africa and America. The name fir is derived from the Old English *furh* and German *fohre* and in Germany the tree was also a symbol of prosperity. Long before Prince Albert introduced Christmas trees to England in the late nineteenth century, the evergreen leaves and branches of firs were used in pagan and Christian festivals.

The use of evergreen trees to symbolise eternal life was a custom of ancient Egypt and in China. A symbol of truth and forthrightness because it grows straight to the sky, for the druids the fir was one of nine sacred woods burned for a sabbath fire. Grouped together, fir trees were a symbol of friendship, promise and the renewal of spring following the dark days of winter.

The Celts were not the only ones to recognize the fir's ability to outlive most other trees. The Romans used Fir Trees to decorate their temples at the festival of Saturnalia. Christians use it as a sign of everlasting life with God. Like other evergreens, some associated the tree with the idea of strength and protection. Alonquian native American tribes used its foliage for purification and warding off evil spirits. And in ancient Greece people believed the fir represented sadness, for legend held that Pitys was wooed by Pan and Boreas, the North

Wind. When Pitys rejected Boreas, he blew her over a cliff. Pan discovered her, but could not heal her. The only way she would live was to turn her into a fir tree. Hence forth she shed tear drops of resin, especially when blown by the wind.

During the Middle Ages fir trees would be planted outside the homes of newly married couples in his homeland in order to bring happiness. There they were decorated with apples, nuts and sweets and, with the approach of the eighteenth century, were illuminated with candles.

The evergreen fir tree has traditionally been used to celebrate winter festivals (pagan and Christian) for thousands of years. Pagans used branches of it to decorate their homes during the winter solstice, as it made them think of the spring to come. The Romans used Fir Trees to decorate their temples at the festival of Saturnalia. Christians use it as a sign of everlasting life with God.

Nobody knows when firs were first used as Christmas trees. The first documented use of a tree at Christmas and New Year celebrations is argued between the cities of Tallinn in Estonia and Riga in Latvia. Both claim that they had the first trees; Tallinn in 1441 and Riga in 1510. Trees were put up by the 'Brotherhood of Blackheads', an association of local unmarried merchants, ship owners, and foreigners in Livonia (now Estonia and Latvia). Little is known about either tree apart from that they were put in the town square, were dance around by the Brotherhood of Blackheads and were then set on fire.

In the modern age we still love to decorate our fir trees at Christmas and use their woody, earthy oil in air fresheners, incense and bath oils. Homeopaths use it to help fight sore throat and respiratory infections, muscle aches and arthritis.

'Christmas tree at Windsor Castle', wood engraving by J.L. Williams, 1848.

FRANKINCENSE

THE FRANKINCENSE TREE is a scraggy, hardy tree with white or green star-shaped flowers and spikey leaves. It can be found in Oman, Southern Yemen, Dhofar and Somalia where it is able to survive in very harsh conditions, on steep, rocky slopes and in poor soil.

All frankincense trees belong to the Burseraceae family, named after the sixteenth-century botanist Joachim Burser. The Arabian frankincense tree, *Boswella sacra* was named after John Boswell, a Scottish physician and uncle of James Boswell who wrote the celebrated biography of Samuel Johnson.

As the name 'sacra' suggests, the tree is revered in many Eastern cultures and considered to be a holy tree on account of the syrupy resin cut from the bark of the tree used in perfumes and burned as incense for millennia. It is also referred to many times both in the Old and New Testaments, where it is renowned for being one of the gifts brought by the Magi to the baby Jesus. It might also be argued that the tree changed the Arabian peninsula. Ships would come to collect and trade frankincense, and bring technology and ideas with them.

The name frankincense itself means 'incense that is pure' and as such it is believed to connect directly with the Gods. Droplets known as tears harden over time, turning from milky white to red and golden, as if the tree is weeping as it releases its divine nectar.

Frankincense, or olibanum, has been traded in the Arabian Peninsula, North Africa and Somalia for over five thousand years. Camel trains along the great Silk Routes crossing East to West and in Arabic it was known as *lubaan*. Herodotus, writing in the fifth century BC wrote it was difficult to collect on account of the great numbers of 'flying snakes' guarding the trees. The ancient Egyptians used frankincense for embalming. A mural depicting sacks of frankincense adorns the temple of the Eqyptian Queen Hatsheput dating from around 1458 BC.

Today frankincense is a key ingredient in perfumes, used in aromatherapy and skin care. It is also edible and employed in traditional medicines in Asia and Africa for digestive problems and skin complaints.

Only four main species of the tree produce true frankincense, which in turn is grouped into different grades according to its quality, but recent research shows that tree populations are in decline, partly due to over-exploitation. Research led by Dutch scientist Professor Frans Bongers of Wageningen University in Holland showed that commercial Boswellia was in danger of extinction. Trees across Ethiopia, where most commercial frankincense originates, are dying at an alarming rate. Demand is falling, but the price of frankincense is rising. Farmers are having to use a greater land area for the same yield. Frankincense is a very small crop by world standards, with Ethiopia exporting around 5,000 tons per year: mostly to China for use in medicines and perfumes. The entire Catholic Church uses just 50 tons a year.

Single-handedly, Boswellia has played a major role in the modernity of the Arabian people. Maybe it's time we gave something back to the tree.

GINKGO

GINKGO BILOBA IS an ancient tree found in fossils dating back 270 million years. The tree is native to China, where some trees growing today are thought to be over 1500 years old. Its name is derived from the Japanese word ginkyo, literally 'silver apricot'. Their seeds are pollinated by male sperm cells carried by the wind from the catkins of male trees onto the female tree.

The first European to discover the Gingko was Engelbert Kämpfer on the island of Deshima where he was cultivating a botanical garden. In 1716 he wrote of his discovery in his book, *The History of Japan*. Ginkgos are renowned for their unusual twin-lobed leaves, as the name suggests - 'biloba' after the Latin bis, or two and 'loba'. The Chinese have used the leaves in medicine for centuries. Extract of the leaf is said to enhance brain function and prevent memory loss. So unusual is the leaf that the German writer Johan Wolfgang von Goethe wrote a poem about the ginkgo in his garden.

Ginkgo trees have demonstrated an extraordinary ability to recover after extreme devastation. In Hiroshima six trees between one and two kilometres from the 1945 atomb bomb explosion were charred but able to survive the blast, although all other plants were destroyed. The six trees are still alive.

'The gingko biloba in John Bertram's garden', a gift from William Hamilton, a neighbour and well-known botanist who introduced the tree to North America in 1785.

HANDKERCHIEF

THE HANDKERCHIEF OR dove tree is a medium-sized tree in the dogwood family *Cornacae* that is native to central and southwest China. It is known for its striking white floppy bracts that surround its small purple flowers from a distance resemble ghostly handkerchiefs.

Davidia involucrata, the Latin name for the extraordinary handkerchief is derived after Father Armand David, a French Vincentian missionary and naturalist living in China in the nineteenth century first described the tree in 1869. *Involucrata* means 'cover' or 'sheath' and refers to the large white bracts that cover the tree when it is in full bloom. Father David sent specimens to Paris of the tree with flowers that 'quivered like doves perching on the branches'. He was also the first Westerner to describe numerous flora and fauna, including a swan, a lily, a species of deer and the giant panda.

The handkerchief tree is arguably the most significant botanical discovery in nineteenth-century China and was once thought to be so important it was considered the Holy Grail of exotic flora. To this end, in 1881 the Irish plant hunter and physician Augustine Henry was riding his pony through a river gorge in the Yangtse Ichang in Hubei when he spotted a solitary handkerchief tree in full bloom. It was a spectacular sight and immediately he sent specimens to Kew Gardens in London. Handkerchiefs require humid conditions and plentifal rainfall levels, and unfortunately the seeds did not germinate.

Henry spent much of his twenty years in China collecting plants, but it was not until 1901 that another young botanist named Ernest Henry Wilson was charged by the powerful nurseryman Sir Harry Veitch to locate Henry's tree. 'Do not dissipate time, energy or money on anything else,' wrote Veitch in their contract. Wilson set off to the remote Yunann region, escaping local bandits and surviving a near fatal illness in his pursuit of the rare tree. Upon arrival at the site of Henry's tree discovered it had been felled to make timber for building.

Fortunately he found an entire grove growing not far away, but his rollercoaster journey was not yet over. On his return his boat overturned in a rocky river and he almost drowned. Fortunately he lived to tell the tale – and managed to rescue his previous *Davidia* specimens.

The handkerchief tree was subsequently introduced from China to Europe and America in 1904, but it is still a rare treat to see a handkerchief in full flower. It is a rather slow-growing tree and takes around ten to twelve years before it begins to flourish. Good examples are relatively rare in Britain, because the handkerchief is a sensitive tree and requires certain weather conditions and soil quality to flourish.

Some magnificent examples of mature handkerchiefs can be viewed during late spring at Kew Gardens in London, the grounds of Speke Hall in Liverpool and those of Sizergh Castle in Cumbria. One stands in the grounds of Leeds University's Oxley Hall and another planted in 1906 is to be found in Trebah Garden near Falmouth in Cornwall.

HAWTHORN

THE HAWTHORN TREE has more myths and associations with ancient tradition than almost any other tree. A powerful supernatural force for good and evil, the advent of May blossom heralded the end of winter and beginning of summer in many cultures.

Hawthorn remains the only British tree named after the month in which it blooms. The May tree, as it is commonly known, has been celebrated in countryside May festivals for centuries, is blossoms used in garlands and placed on front doorsteps to bring good fortune.

Celtic mythology is strewn with tales of hawthorns inhabited and guarded by fairies. Hawthorns have always been considered to be special and therefore never cut down for fear of upsetting their tiny guardians. In Ireland few superstitious people will speak of the fairy tree out of a mixture of fear and respect and even fewer would ever remove or damage a hawthorn standing alone. Work was once interrupted on the main road from Limerick to Galway because a fairy tree stood in its path. The road had to be rerouted and construction was delayed for ten years. There have also been numerous sightings of an ancient ghost thought to reappear in Tyrone after the felling of a fairy tree there.

Places where hawthorn trees grow have been considered sacred sites, such as that of Westminster Abbey, which was once known as Thorney Island after the hawthorns that grew upon the surrounding land.

Hawthorns have always been associated with Christ's crown of thorns. The most famous hawthorn in Britain is the sacred Thorn of Glastonbury. Legend holds that Joseph of Arimathea arrived at Glastonbury Tor with his disciples. It is said that he was carrying two vessels containing the blood and sweat of Jesus and that where he marked the ground with his staff a thorn tree grew up on the spot.

The hawthorn to which that story pertains must be long gone, but a few of its descendants stand in the surrounding area and a sprig is taken from one of these standing outside St John's Church and sent to the Queen every Christmas to decorate her breakfast table.

In the Middle Ages the leaves of hawthorn were eaten and the blossom and berries used to make wine and jellies. The strong wood was used to make tools and utensils and in gardens the hawthorn was a favourite for making hedges. The name 'hawthorn' is derived from the Old English 'hagathorn', literally 'hedge thorn'.

During the Black Death hawthorn became a symbol of bad luck if brought into a home. The strong, fetid smell of the flowers was said to be a harbinger of the plague itself. Indeed, they were not entirely mistaken. Botanists later discovered that the chemical trimethylamine present in the flowers is one of the first formed in decaying animal tissue.

Despite its association with death, hawthorn is believed by some to contain life-giving properties. Herbalists today use it to treat low and high blood pressure, chest pain and congestive heart failure.

'

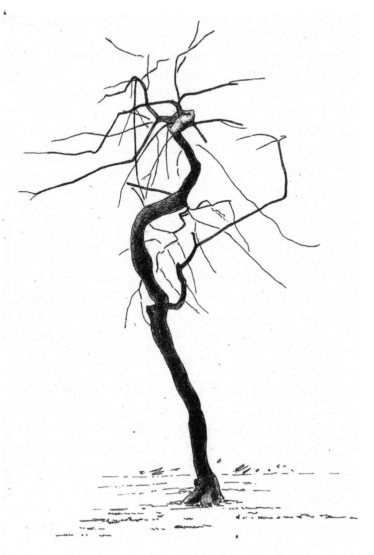

Hawthorn (*Crataegus*); tree with no leaves. Pen drawing.

HAZEL

THE NAME HAZEL is derived from the Anglo-Saxon word 'haesel', meaning 'cap' or 'hat' and which originally signified a baton of authority. The common hazel, *Corylus avellana* means 'helmet' in Greek. Both refer to the small cluster of leaves over the nut, which forms a protective cover. The Gaelic term for hazel is 'coll' and the name recurs in many places in Ireland and Western Scotland today, such as in the isle of Coll and Bar Calltuin in Argyllshire. It also appears in the name of Clan Colquhoun, whose motif is the hazel.

In Celtic mythology the tree is regarded as a guardian, both of man and the planet. Many early Irish tales describe poets and seers as 'gaining nuts of wisdom', a metaphor for heightened states of consciousness, although the more literally-minded have argued that this expression could refer to a potent brew made from hazels that had psychotropic effects. There are numerous references to drinking 'hazelmead' in early Irish literature and many references to Scottish druids eating hazel-nuts to gain prophetic powers. Gaelic tradition holds that wherever the hazel tree grows, the earth around is sacred. The hazel tree is a symbol of wisdom and inspiration.

Legend has it that nine hazel trees once stood around a pool known as the Well of Wisdom where sacred salmon, the Salmon of Knowledge, swam. In some accounts, the hazel-nuts cause bubbles of 'mystic inspiration' to form on the surface of the streams that flow down from the well; in others, the Salmon of Knowledge and Inspiration eat the nuts and send the husks floating downstream; those that eat the nuts (or the salmon) gain poetic and prophetic powers. Fin McCool, a great hero of ancient Gaelic tales, is believed to have cooked a fish from this pool whilst he was still a young apprentice. Some of the juice spattered onto his thumb, which he instinctively sucked to cool, thereby imbibing the fish's wisdom.

In Norse mythology the hazel was known as the Tree of Knowledge and was sacred to Thor; the Romans held it sacred to Mercury, who – especially in his Greek form, Hermes, was the personification of intelligence. Hermes' magic rod may have been made from hazel.

Elsewhere in folklore, the hazel, along with the apple and hawthorn, is a tree often found at the border between the worlds where magical things may happen. In the Scots ballad, Hind Etin, the title is the name of a spirit who guards the hazels of a sacred tree. The May Margret goes to the wood for nuts, and unwisely gathers his nuts:

Hazels, particularly common hazels, are cultivated for their nuts, said to bring good fortune. They are full of protein and for centuries were used to make breads. On Halloween, also known as Nutcrack Night hazels were eaten and fortune told. A worm in a nut signified bad times ahead. Even the hazel's leaves were believed to bring prosperity, so much so that they were fed to cattle to increase their milk yield.

Hazel wood is extremely pliable and has long been used for making walking sticks, baskets and the frames of coracle boats. In Medieval times it was used in wattle for making houses and for holding down thatch on roofs.

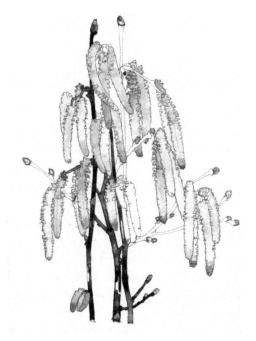

'Hazel lambs tails, Walberswick,' Charles & Margaret Mackintosh, 1915.

HOLLY

No spear no trust, no shield against the shock of battle,
But in one hand a solitary branch of holly
That shows greenest as the groves are leafless.

WHEN THE ANONYMOUS author of *Sir Gawain and the Green Knight* wrote these words in the fourteenth century the holly tree's cultural significance had already been established for centuries. In heraldry it symbolized truth. In Paganism it was believed to protect against evil spirits. People brought holly leaves into their homes to provide shelter from the cold for the fairy folk who, it was said, would in turn bless the house and all who lived there.

In pagan times, holly was thought to be a male plant and ivy a female plant. *The Holly and the Ivy* is a traditional British Christmas carol which refers to these old fertility myths. The holly tree was also a fertility charm. Sprigs were worn to help conception. If a holly bore no berries it would signal infertility upon the inhabitants of a village for a year. Holly leaves were also a harbinger of good fortune. A holly crown was worn for luck and newborn babies were bathed in water that had been steeped in holly leaves. Legend held that the holly was the evergreen twin of the oak. While the oak king oversaw the summer, the holly king, a giant wielding a great holly bush as a club, guarded the dark winter months. And in nordic cultures the tree was associated with thunder Gods such as Thor and Taranis. A holly tree was planted near a house to help ward off lightning strikes as it was believed that a holly tree could not be struck by lightening – making the tree a safe place to shelter during a storm.

Long before the nineteenth century the European holly tree, or *ilex aquifolium*, carried religious associations. The Middle English name for the tree was 'holyn' and in old German it was 'hulin' – holy, used in wreaths, decorations and sung about in songs and carols. Its glossy, spiky leaves were of major symbolic significance in Christianity, particularly at Christmas, a reminder of the crown of thorns worn by Christ, and the berries were a sign of his blood.

In Scotland the Gaelic term for holly, 'chuillin', is found in many place names, such as the town of Cuilen in Banff-shire to that of Chuillin in Ross-shire. It is still considered unlucky to fell a holly tree, just as it was in 1861 when the Duke of Argyll had a potential road redirected to avoid cutting down an old holly on his estate. Today, most holly trees, even old one, are moderately sized trees that can grow up to twenty metres tall and live for three hundred years.

Hollies are either male or females and are pollinated by insects, mostly bees. One male tree can pollinate many females. *Ilex*, the botanical name for holly was awarded by Carl Linnaeus because the considered the leaves to be similar to those of the oak. However, many varieties of holly have smooth leaves or smoother leaves higher up the tree. The wood of the holly is strong. Holly wood could steer horses better than any other wood and in the days of horse-drawn carriages and carts it was used for coachmen's whips.

'Holly tree', taken from *De Historia* by Leonhart Fuchs.

HORNBEAM

THE EUROPEAN HORNBEAM, or Carpinus betalus, is native to Western Asia and central southern Europe. It belongs to the birch family. A small tree, with silvery pale trunk and branches, its leaves are often confused with those of the beech tree. It is a strong tree. As John Evelyn wrote, it grows tall and sturdy, 'so as not to be usurped by the winds'.

The hornbeam takes its name from the hardness of its wood. So tough is it that in past centuries it was likened to horn. As John Gerard wrote, 'The wood in time waxeth so hard that the toughness and hardness of it may rather be compared to a horn unto wood'. The Old English 'beam' means 'tree'.

The genus name, *carpinus* actually relates to the Celtic 'carr', meaning 'wood' and 'pen' or 'head', since hornbeam was used for yokes for oxen. It is also a beautiful grain and a favourite choice for making musical instruments, for example the hammers of piano keys, as well as pulleys, windmill cogs and pulleys. Hornbeam also makes excellent firewood.

In medieval England a tonic made from hornbeam was said to relieve exhaustion and leaves were used as wound dressings. To this day, hornbeam is still an ingredient in Bach flower remedies.

'European hornbeam', Washington DC, taken in 1920.

HORSE CHESTNUT

T HE COMMON HORSE chestnut tree, *Aesculus hippocastanum*, is not simply a tree for autumn when its hand-like leaves turn scarlet and brown. Throughout the year it is an iconic landmark of the British countryside, common to parks, gardens and village greens.

Some scholars argue that the name horse chestnut was coined when the Flemish ambassador to Turkey named Ogier Chislain de Busteq, when visiting the court of Suleiman the Magnificent, spotted Turkish soldiers offering fruit to their horses. Others believe that the prefix 'horse' is a corruption of the Welsh *gwres*, meaning hot, fierce, or pungent as opposed to the mild, sweet variety. Horse Chestnuts were fed to horses in the East as a stimulant and to make their coat shine. The leaf-scars on the twigs have the shape of a horseshoe, including the nail holes.

In ancient Greece the chestnut was popular and chestnuts from a tree known as *Sardis glans*, or 'Sardis acorn', were eaten in honour of the God Zeus. Indeed the Greek name *castanea* is derived from Castonis, a town where many chestnuts grew. The tree was introduced to Europe in 1576 and to Britain in 1633 from western Asia and was subsequently planted extensively by landscape gardeners throughout the country.

It was not until about 200 years later that the fruits of the horse chestnut trees were used to play 'conkers'. Before that, the game was played with hazel or cobnuts or snail shells. The game is believed to have first taken place on the Isle of Wight in 1848. Originally it was played with conch shells, snail shells and later cobnuts. A variant of the game was later played with hazelnuts, on strings.

Conkers have also been carried in the pocket to help prevent piles and rheumatism, and used in wardrobes to keep away moths. According to a letter which appeared in the *Daily Telegraph*, conkers are an effective way to keep spiders out of the house: conkers, placed in the corners of a room and behind pieces of furniture, reduce the number of spiders venturing into the room. However, over a period, the conkers dry up and lose their efficacy

During World War I a wide appeal was made for people to collect the seeds, which were then used to produce acetone, a solvent in the production of weaponry. However, the plan sadly failed and the only factory producing acetone closed its doors after just three months.

Nowadays the Horse Chestnut is a popular ornamental tree in parks, gardens, town and village squares, churchyards and in streets. The tree flowers abundantly from April to mid-May and the white and sometimes red flower-spikes are popularly known as 'candles', since they seem to light up the tree.

JUNIPER

THE JUNIPER IS a member of the cypress family and is native to many countries in the Northern Hemisphere, from the Arctic to Africa and Central Asia. There are around sixty-seven species and sub-species of the conifer, whose cones are so unusually fleshy and merged that they seem more like berries and are consequently known as such.

The common juniper, *J.communis*, has been widespread in Europe since the Roman period. Indeed, juniper berries have been discovered in many Egyptian tombs, including that of Tutankhamun. The Greeks recorded using juniper berries as a stimulant for athletes competing at Olympus because they believed the juniper increased stamina. The Romans substituted cheap juniper for expensive black pepper imported from India. Pliny the Elder wrote in his *Natural History*, 'Pepper is adulterated with juniper berries, which have the property to a marvelous degree of assuming the pungency of pepper.'

Juniper smoke is highly aromatic, and in ancient times it was used for the ritual purification of temples. The smoke was said to aid clairvoyance, and continued to be burned for purification and to stimulate contact with the otherworld at the autumn Samhain fire festival at the beginning of the Celtic year. In central Europe juniper smoke played a part in the spring-time cleansing and casting out of witchcraft. Juniper was also burned during outbreaks of the Plague, and in

Scotland the disease could be dispelled by fumigating the house with juniper smoke while its occupants were inside, after which the house was aired and the occupants revived with whisky!

Juniper berries have been used medicinally for centuries. In the seventeenth century the herbalist Nicholas Culpeper prescribed them in the treatment of asthma and sciatica, as well as to hasten childbirth. Some cultures, such as American Indians, used them to treat loss of appetite and even as a female contraceptive, others as a treatment to counter diabetes. But perhaps most famously the physician Francois du Bois is known for distilling the berries in spirits in order to produce a diuretic remedy. The mixture was a hit and from then on the alcoholic spirit gin, from the French *genièvre* or 'juniper', became a staple. In the nineteenth century Highland juniper bushes were prolific enough for their berries to be collected by the bagful and taken to the Inverness and Aberdeen markets to be exported to the Dutch gin distillers.

Juniper's use in cooking is many and varied. In the Medieval period the berries were ground and added to sauces and especially to game dishes to add a bitter, spicy flavour, and were used to flavour bread and cakes in the north of England. The berries are still used to flavour other alcoholic beverages such as a Swedish health beer and a French beer-like drink called *genevrette* made from equal amounts of juniper berries and barley. Juniper berries are regarded as a spice to give a sharp, clean flavor to many meat dishes, particularly in North European cuisine.

The cypress and juniper trees of the Rocky Mountain region (1915).

LARCH

THE EUROPEAN LARCH, *L.decidua*, thrives in high mountainous regions and is one of only a few trees able to grow in the tundra. Scholars believe it was carried to Britain by the botanist and gardener John Tradescant the Elder in 1618, when he was charged by George Villiers, Duke of Buckingham, to travel to Russia, the Levant and Algiers in search of new plants.

One of the primary mountain-side trees of Europe, the larch has become a common forestry tree. In winter few other trees look as scraggy, as unkempt as the larch does. It is a deciduous conifer and so loses its needle-like leaves so that rough bare branches thick with small cones disguise the often, graceful lines of the downswept boughs. In early spring tufts of bright green needles revitalise its appearance, and if one looks carefully, amazingly sculptural little flowers can be seen just as the green appears. Male flowers are yellow-orange, female flowers to become the cones, are deep crimson crowns spaced along each branch. In autumn, the whole tree turns copper-orange and in the late autumnal sunlight, a burnished brass.

Larch has been a sacred tree of the druids and ruler of the winter solstice for centuries. One myth holds that *sälingen*, the 'blessed spirits', lived in the tree. The wood was heavily used in pagan rituals, especially cremations, where it was burned in the 'sag' or 'cremation stack'.

Larch also plays an important role in Sami and Siberian

mythology where it takes the place of the ash as the world tree. Shamans use larch wood to rim their ceremonial drums. The smoke from burning larch is said to ward off evil. Larch is used for protection and to induce visions.

Larch wood is strong and knot free and has always been in huge demand for building and fencing. Along with other conifers it was used in Roman times for ship building, after Julius Caesar chanced upon it during one of his raids. A generation later larch became the key building material in the construction of a palace for the Emperor Augustus.

Larch wood is rich in resin, which remains liquid when heated and this particular quality has made the wood a favourite for boat and ship building, where it was ideal in the production of pitch and Venetian turpentine used to waterproof ships.

Nowadays three types of larch are to be found in Great Britain. Apart from the European larch, is the Japanese, or *L.kaempferi*, introduced in around 1861. Later on a hybrid of the European and Japanese species is thought to have been introduced at Dunkeld.

The Parent larch is thought to be one of the largest examples of the tree still alive. Planted in Perthshire in 1738, it was a gift to Duke James Atholl from a Mr Menzies of Megany in Glenlyon. Another great larch, the Kailzie larch is said to be even older. This tree is situated near Peebles and is said to have been planted in 1725 by Sir James Nasmyth of Posso whilst visiting his friend of Kailzie. Its trunk extends almost sixteen feet in girth.

'Larch tree', ink drawing by James Ward, 1843.

LEMON

L EMON TREES are believed to have originated in Assam in India. Scholars have discovered that they were transported to Italy during the Roman period and were subsequently introduced to Persia, Iraq and Egypt as far back as 700 AD. In China they were known as 'limung'.

In Greek mythology the lemon tree was known as the 'tree of the golden apples ", in a comparison with the apple tree. The lemon tree was represented in mythology as donor of the immortality and considered to be a symbol of fecundity. For it it was a custom that was appearing this fruit in the wedding ceremonies. Renowned for its cleansing properties, staffs of priests were made of lemon wood. Its fruit was a gift of the goddess Gea to the goddess Hera and the god Zeus. The tree was placed in the Garden of the Hespérides and was guarded by a dragoon – serpent of hundred heads called Ladón.

By 1000 AD the fruit of the lemon tree was available throughout the Middle East along with citrons, a fruit not unlike the lemon. Cultivation of the lemon tree, with its thinner-skinned fruit, spread along with trade and Islam in that region. Crusaders fighting holy battles in the twelfth century brought exotic lemons back home with them to Britain and where they were the preserve of the rich due to their high price. Our name for them is derived from the Old French 'limon', the Italian 'limone' and in turn the Persian and Arabic 'lemoon'.

In 1493 Christopher Columbus carried lemon seeds to the Americas and Hispaniola and with the Spanish conquest of the region popularity of the tree and its sharp, refreshing fruit widened. The gentler climes of southern Europe proved perfect conditions for the lemon to thrive and the tree was planted widely in ornamental gardens.

In 1747 a young Scottish naval physician named James Lind made a crucial medicinal discovery regarding the fruit of the lemon tree when he found that sailors suffering from scurvy benefited greatly from drinking lemon juice. At the time vitamin C had not yet even been identified.

Today there are several species of lemon tree all offering slightly different fruit. For example, the Meyer, named after Frank N Meyer who introduced it to America in 1908 is milder and thin-skinned, whereas the Ponderosa is large and with a thicker skin. The Eureka or Four Seasons is the most common because it is available all year long whatever the season. The Italian variety Femminello St Teresa is traditionally used for making *limoncello*.

Lemon tree (Citrus limon); branch with fruit and flowers.

LINDEN

THE LINDEN, LIME, or tilia tree is a large deciduous tree commonly to be found in many parts of Europe. 'Lime' is from the Middle English 'lind' meaning 'made from lime wood'. The bark of a linden contains particularly strong fibre. Excavations by archaeologists date its use in clothing to the Bronze Age. A coppice of linden trees in Gloucestershire is thought to be two thousand years old and in Nuremberg a tree is said to have been planted by the wife of Henry of Orange around 1000 AD.

Various myths and superstitions sprang up about the powers of the linden in ancient times. Homer, Horace, Vigil and Pliny all wrote of the benefits of the tree and one of Ovid's heroines, Philemon, even became one. According to Herodotus, Scythian diviners and soothsayers used the leaves of the linden to tell fortunes; in Baltic folklore sacrifices were offered to the tree asking for fertility; and in Germany the linden has always been the tree of lovers and believed to bring luck.

Laima, the goddess of fate in Lithuania, is associated with the lime. Laima's dwelling was a lime-tree, where she made her decisions as a cuckoo; and the linden was a particularly highly symbolic and hallowed tree to German mythology. Originally, local communities assembled not only to celebrate and dance under a linden tree, but to hold their judicial thing meetings there in order to restore justice and peace. So widely held was the belief that the tree would help unearth the truth that the linden became associated with jurisprudence even after and verdicts in rural Germany were frequently returned under the linden until the Age of Enlightenment.

In the *Nibelungenlied*, a medieval German work ultimately based on spoken tradition recounting events amongst the Germanic tribes in the fifth and sixth centuries, Siegfried gains his invulnerability by bathing in the blood of a dragon. While he did so, a single linden leaf sticks to him, leaving a spot on his body untouched by the blood and he thus has a single point of vulnerability.

Still today, in Eastern European countries and particularly in Poland, the linden is considered a sacred tree. In the Czech Republic it is a national emblem. Linden flowers are used in traditional medicine to treat everything from flu and colds to poor digestion and sleep disorders.

The most notable street in Berlin, Germany is called Unter den Linden, named after the trees lining the avenue. In German folklore, the linden tree is the tree of lovers. Hohenlinden or 'High linden' is a community in the upper Bavarian district of Ebersberg in which the Battle of Hohenlinden took place;

As well as being an ancient tree, the wood is lightweight, dense and so soft that during the Middle Ages it was used for shields and carvings. Later it was a favourite for making puppets and its excellent acoustic properties have lent it to being used for wind instruments and drum shells.

'Unter den Linden', showing a boulevard in Berlin
by J Strindbeck, 1691.

'Under the Linden Tree', a medieval village festival in Germany depicting
an entertainer performing under a magnificent linden tree.

MACADAMIA

THE MACADEMIA TREE is a rainforest tree native to eastern Australia. For thousands of years before Europeans settled in the region, aborigines ate the seeds of the evergreen that they named the 'kindal kindal', the 'boombera', the 'jindall' and the 'boppal'. Macademia nuts even then were considered a delicacy and were traded between tribes or given as gifts. Aboriginal women collected them and removed the husks and cracked open the nuts with stones. Aboriginal legend held that the time had once came for the tribes to decide who would look after their land and protect it. Someone was sent to the north and someone else to look south, but when it came to the mountains in the east no one wanted to travel that far. One, named Boppal, volunteered for the task and as he prepared to walk the long path a lizard crept into his pack.

Along the way, Boppal fell. Seeking to help him, the lizard asked a rock wallaby what they should do. The rock wallaby offered to fetch water, but he could not reach the water with his small arms. The kangaroo helped him. Boppal needed food, and this time the lizard asked the cockatoo, who flew out over the mountain and collected nuts. At last all the animals made a fire to help Boppal, and the villagers, seeing its smoke, ran to rescue Boppal. From that day they called the mountain Boppal's mountain, the lizard Boppal's lizard and the nuts Boppal's nuts. Still today in the Gympie region of Australia seasonal feasts of the boppal are held.

It was not until 1850 that a European discovered the tree in Queensland. Dr Ferdinand von Mueller duly named it after his friend, the Scottish physician Dr John MacAdam, although the latter never tasted its seeds. He died soon after from an injury whilst sailing to New Zealand. Walter Hill, who had accompanied Dr Mueller on his trip planted the first cultivated macademia tree in Brisbane Botanical Gardens and initially believed the nuts to be poisonous. Only after one of his assistants accidentally ate the nuts with no ill effects did he change his mind. Soon orchards were being planted throughout New South Wales and in 1881 William Purvis introduced macadamia trees to Hawaii as a windbreak for the sugar cane crops growing there and in 1922 Ernst Van Tassel formed the Hawaiian Macadamia Nut Co in Hawaii. Tassel leased 75 acres on Round Top in Honolulu, Nut Ridge and began a macadamia nut orchard, Hawaii's first macadamia seed farm. It was not until 1964 that Macadamia Nuts Pty Ltd opened Australia's first purpose-built processing plant at Slacks Creek, near Brisbane, Queensland.

Macadamia nuts are still in high demand, and nowadays most commercially macadamias are grown in South Africa. The nuts are among the hardest to crack on earth, able to resist even the blow of a hammer. Research shows they can total and LDL cholesterol levels. Although they are toxic to dogs, humans have no adverse effects when eating them. They are a rich source of essential nutrients including vitamin B6, thiamin, manganese, iron, magnesium and phosphorus.

MAHOGANY

THERE ARE THREE species of mahogany tree belonging to the genus *Swietenia*. They are the Honduran mahogany (*S.macrophylla*), the West Indian or Cuban mahogany, (*S.mahagoni*) and the Pacific mahogany, or *S.humilis*. However, prior to the nineteenth century any differentiation between them was not acknowledged.

The tree was named *Swietenia* after Dr Gerard van Swieten, a Dutch physician to the Empress Maria Theresa of Austria. Swieten was a prominent doctor, founding an important school of medicine, a laboratory and a botanical garden in Vienna. The garden proved so successful that its director, Nikolaus von Jacquin, named the mahogany in honour of Swieten, having seen the tree whilst on his travels to the West Indies in 1757.

Mahogany trees have grown mainly in the British-occupied islands of the West Indies and in the Spanish territories where the tree was known as *caoba*. Some scholars argue that the word mahogany is a derivative of the word in the African Yoruba language, *m'dganwo*, used to refer to a similar tree, the *khaya*. It is believed that when African slaves were transported to Jamaica, they identified the trees as those they knew from their homeland. Others dispute the story and say there is no evidence to confirm that it is true.

Mahogany wood is renowned for its fine, evenly grained texture, strength, beauty and deep, rich colour, but it was only truly discovered by Europeans following the Spanish conquest of the Americas. In 1721 the British tax laws on imported timber relaxed. West Indian timbers including mahogany became much more readily available and the trade in the wood soared along with demand. Mahogany quickly became a favourite of the best craftsmen. Thomas Chippendale used it among others for making cabinets, chairs and tables.

From the 1820s mahogany from all these areas was imported into Europe and North America, with the bulk going to Britain. In Central America British loggers moved northwest towards Mexico and south into Guatemala. Other areas of Central America as far south as Panama also began to be exploited. Trade in American mahogany probably reached a peak in the last quarter of the 19th century. Figures are not available for all countries, but Britain alone imported more than 80,000 tons in 1875,

In 1907 the total of mahogany from all sources imported into Europe was 159,830 tons, of which 121,743 tons were from West Africa. By this time mahogany from Cuba, Haiti and other West Indian sources had become increasingly difficult to obtain in commercial sizes, and by the late twentieth century Central American and even South American mahogany wood was equally rare and sought after. However, not everyone appreciates the value of the mahogany tree. In the Philippines environmentalists are calling for an end to the planting of mahogany because of its negative impact on the environment and wildlife, including possibly causing soil acidification and no net benefit to wildlife

'The beach at Axim, with mahogany logs', monograph taken from *Nine Years at the Gold Coast*, by Dennis Kemp, 1898.

MANGO

MANGO TREES HAVE been grown in Asia for millennia, originally found in East India, Burma and the Andaman Islands near the Bay of Bengal. Around the fifth century BC Buddhist monks are thought to have introduced them to Eastern Asia and to Malaysia and Islamic traders took the mango to the Middle East and from there the Portuguese brought the tree to Brazil and the West Indies. Chinese traveler Hwen T'sang visited India in the first half of the seventh century AD and took the mango back to his home. The Chinese were delighted and began cultivating the magnificent evergreen tree that stands up to 100 feet tall with beautiful, thick, shiny, leathery pointed leaves that grow 8 to 14 inches long.

Symmetrical in shape, the mango tree is a beautiful ornamental that is also appreciated for its cooling shade. In India the mango is a symbol of love and many classical Sanskrit poets sang its praises. By the sixteenth century the mango had become so revered in India that royalty hoarded the groves solely for the rajas and nawabs. Portuguese explorers carried the mango further East and to West Africa and Brazil. The Mogul Emperor Akbar is believed to have planted an orchard of 100,000 mango trees in Darbhanga, because he loved the tree and believed it to bring good fortune.

Hindu culture holds that the tree is sacred. Some even believe that it can grant wishes. So holy is the mango that

Buddha was said to have found tranquility beneath its branches. The goddess Ambika was depicted sitting beneath the tree and Lord Ganesha holding a ripe mango, symbol of perfection. Still today the goddess Saraswati is offered mango blossoms as a blessing. Mango leaves decorate archways and doors in Indian homes, particularly during Ponggol, the Hindu New Year, said to bless the house and all who dwell there. At weddings eating mangoes ensured fertility and the birth of a male child is celebrated by hanging mango leaves.

Since ancient times the seeds and fruit of the mango have been used in Ayurvedic medicine. Tea made from the leaves treated all manner of diseases, from infections of the mouth, diabetes and tiredness to diarrhea, dysentery, cholesterol and memory loss. Mangiferin found in the stem bark of the mango is even believed by some to inhibit tumour growth in certain cancers.

Today, India's main fruit crop is still the mango that outnumbers all the country's other fruit crops. In Tamil, the language of Southeastern India, the mango received its original name *mancay* that later evolved into *manga* by the Portuguese. Mango fruits are fundamental to the export market of both India and Pakistan. The wood, although susceptible to fungi and insects, is used in furniture-making and for musical instruments such as the ukulele.

'Mango tree and creatures who dwell there,' taken from the
Illustrated London News, 1872.

MAPLE

IN THE FOURTEENTH century Geoffrey Chaucher wrote of 'the mapul' in his *Knight's Tale*, although the tree was not yet known in Britain. Centuries later when the poet John Clare described the autumnal beauty of the maple 'with its tassel flowers of green that turn to red, a stag horn shaped seed just spreading out its scalloped leaves' he was writing about an iconic tree that has shaped the landscape in multiple continents.

Fossil evidence shows that maple trees have existed on earth for at least a hundred million years, although archeologists have found that some species vanished during the Ice Age. Today there are 128 species of maple in the Aceraceae family, of which 54 face an uncertain future due to erosion of their natural habitat.

The European maple, *Acer campestre*, literally meaning 'field maple', is the only maple common to Britain. Some say that the Tolpuddle Martyrs met under a maple before they were deported to Australia and that as their ship sailed their leader carried a leaf from that tree pressed into the pages of his Bible. However, most scholars agree that the tree was a sycamore rather than a maple.

The maple tree has always been of great significance to the Alongquian Indians of Northwest America and Western Canada. Maple wood was used to make tools and furniture and the bark formed a traditional medicine. Maple sap was considered a divine gift and many cultural festivals focused around the tree.

The Rocky Mountain maple is still considered one of the sacred medicines of the Najajo tribe. To others, such as the Ojibwe, the tree is a God named Ininati. Children learn about the tree and its sacred sap as soon as they can walk.

In Europe it was believed that maple branches, draped over a front doorway, would prevent bats from flying in. The herbalist Thomas Culpepper prescribed maple bark for strengthening the liver. Gypsies believed maple would attract gold and that eating its seeds would draw love.

The exact origins of maple sugaring are unknown, although there are accounts of the practice dating back to 1557. Native American Indian squaws boiled the sap of the tree and combined it with sugar. By the seventeenth century the native tribes along with French explorers and missionaries were using iron and copper kettles to make large blocks of maple sugar that were both long-lasting and easily transportable.

The American Civil war brought the commercialization of maple sugar and syrup. Dairy farmers often made them off-season to provide extra income. Plantations were begun. Even Thomas Jefferson started a maple plantation in Monticello in 1791.

Unsurprisingly, maples have become emblematic in several countries in which they are so crucial to cultural heritage. The leaf is the national symbol of Canada, just as the Japanese maple or *momiji* leaf has long been a symbol of Hiroshima, depicted in traditional paintings and block prints, bursting with gold, yellow and red.

A hired man on Frank H. Shurtleff farm gathering maple sap from sugar maple trees to make syrup. The Shurtleff farm has about 400 acres and was originally purchased by grandfather in 1840. He raises sheep, cows, cuts lumber and has been making maple syrup for about thirty-five years. Sugaring brings in about one thousand dollars annually. Because of the deep snow this year he only tapped 1000 of his 2000 trees. He expects to make about 300 to 500 gallons this year. North Bridgewater, Vermont.

MONKEY-PUZZLE

THE MONKEY-PUZZLE tree, *Araucaria araucana*, is an evergreen tree native to Southern Chile and Western Argentina also known as the Chilean pine or *peheuén*, although it is only distantly related to the pine family. Renowned for its thick, scaly branches and symmetrical appearance, it is a hardy tree that grows in its natural habitat at around 3000 metres. Evidence exists suggesting that the long necks of sauropod dinosaurs may have evolved to graze the foliage of very tall Araucaria trees during the Jurassic period. Indeed it can live for such a long period of time that the tree has been described as a living fossil.

There are nineteen species in the genus Auracaria, named on account of the native Araucanians who relied upon the seeds or nuts of the tree for survival. The tree was discovered in Chile by Europeans in the 1780s and first introduced into Britain in 1795 when Scottish botanist and naval physician Archibald Menzies was invited to a dinner at the Governor of Chile's residence in Santiago. The story goes that Menzies helped himself to some nuts from a bowl. On the return passage home to Britain he planted the nuts 'in a glazed frame on the quarter deck' on the ship HMS Discover. Miraculously they survived the voyage.

The monkey-puzzle acquired its unusual name when Sir William Molesworth, the owner of a young tree at Pencarrow near Bodwin was showing the specimen to a group of his friends. One of them, a barrister named Charles Austin noted, 'It would puzzle a monkey to climb that'. From then on it was known as the monkey-puzzle and was planted in many Victorian gardens. Today, the reference to primates in the common name is not confined to Great Britain; in France it goes by the more mournful *désespoir des singes*. Instantly recognizable, with its sharp, oval, leathery leaves and curved, sweeping branches, many myths developed around it. Children were told that it was unlucky to talk whilst passing beneath a monkey-puzzle tree. Some very superstitious folk even said that the devil sat in its branches.

Sadly, the monkey-puzzle is now rare in South America, a victim of climate change and the erosion of some of its habitats. However, conservation efforts are being taken. In the two centuries since Menzies pocketed his dinner dessert the monkey puzzle has been under pressure throughout its home range. Deforestation continued through the 1800s and 1900s as Chile industrialised, with Araucaria timber in demand for pit props, paper pulp manufacturing and railway sleepers. Its straight trunk also meant it was particularly suited for use as ships' masts. Although protected by law since 1971 the scale of the felling and milling operations mean the number of trees remaining is a fraction of what it once was, resulting in the tree being classed as vulnerable under the international treaty for endangered species. National Monument status was awarded by the Chilean government in 1990, making it illegal to fell a tree. The toasted nuts are still eaten by those Mapuche communities who close to viable trees.

MULBERRY

IN OVID'S FAMOUS tale of the lovers Pyramus and Thisbe derived from Greek myth the mulberry tree is a metaphor of transformation. Pyramus, arriving beneath a mulberry tree where he has arranged to meet his lover Thisbe commits suicide on discovering she has been killed by a lioness. The splashes of blood stain the previously white berries on the tree and the roots are tinged with a purple dye as if to honour their forbidden love.

The mulberry tree, or *Morus nigra*, in Ovid's story was well known by the Romans, who made wine from its fruit and introduced it to Britain. Its fruit were indeed black or dark purple. A different species of the mulberry, the white-berried *M.alba* was during that period being grown in China, where it was cultivated to feed silkworms that only feed on mulberry leaves. Indeed, legend has it that silk was discovered in the 27th century BC when Empress Xi Ling Shi, wife of the Yellow Emperor, happened to be sitting in the shade of a mulberry tree drinking tea when a silkworm fell into her cup. As the Empress picked the cocoon out of her tea a long, silvery thread began to unwind. Soon afterwards, she commanded a loom to be made to spin the thread into material.

Silk's popularity spread in the East along with the mulberry tree. By the Middle Ages mulberries had long been traded along the silk routes and the trees that fed the worms that made the silk along with them. Henry VIII ordered twenty cherry trees, damsons, red peaches, a fishpond and a mulberry tree for his Chelsea manor and in Shakespeare's day many great mulberries were to be seen in Stratford upon Avon, including one grown from a cutting taken for a tree said to have been planted by Shakespeare himself. The original tree went on to become so celebrated that in the 1800s the owner of Shakespeare's former house, a Reverend Francis Gasvell, became so frustrated with the constant requests he received from visitors wishing to see the tree, that he chopped it down.

King James I was responsible for the planting huge numbers of mulberry trees in Britain. Some say that he wished to wrest the monopoly of the silk trade from the French. At his command a four-acre mulberry garden was planted to the north of what is now Buckingham Palace, tended by the King's Mulberry Men. To this day a street named Mulberry Walk exists near the King's Road in Chelsea.

Ten thousand mulberry trees were imported from Europe and a letter issued ordering the lord lieutenants of the land to purchase and plant the trees at the rate of six shillings per thousand. Sadly, the black mulberries failed within a few years and the British market in silk production with them. Descendants of the original trees can still be seen in the grounds of many stately homes throughout the country, including Charlotte Park in Warwickshire, where a receipt dated 1713 for the purchase and planting of a mulberry tree still exists – as does the tree.

'Mulberry tree', 1919, *American Forestry Association.*

MYRRH

THE MYRRH IS a small, thorny tree native to Yemen, Somalia, Eritrea, Eastern Ethiopia and Oman. It can survive in extremely harsh conditions, tolerating extreme heat and poor soil. It is a member of the Burseracae family and has several species including *Commiphora molmol*, *C abyssinica* and *C myrrha*. The myrrh tree grows to about nine feet and bears small brown fruit and scarlet flowers. Its hairless, roughly-toothed leaves are divided into pairs of oval leaflets.

Myrrh trees have been exploited for millennia to harvest their gum resin, which has a bitter, pungent taste and sweet aroma. The bark is cut to release the gum, which is at first pale, waxy and milky, but slowly hardens and deepens in colour.

The name myrrh is derived from the Arabic *murr*, meaning 'bitter' and the Hebrew *mor* meaning the same. In Old French *mire* meant an apothecary and the bark and gum of the tree were used in the treatment of many ailments.

The Queen of Sheba was said to have given myrrh trees as a gift to the King of Solomon and legend also holds that around the 15th century BC during the rule of Egyptian Pharaoh Thutmose III, Queen Hatshepsut sent an expedition to Africa to collect myrrh trees to surround the temple of the God Amon. The expedition is chronicled on the walls of the temple and the Egyptians believed that Amon was so pleased he awarded Hatshepsut safe passage to the afterlife. Egyptians also used myrrh to repel fleas and for use in healing. Early records reveal that myrrh was a key ingredient in ancient for embalming. It was also a constituent of *ketoret*, the holy incense of the Hebrew Bible and Talmud. It is mentioned many times throughout the Old Testament and in the New Testament as one of the gifts presented by the three Maji to the infant Jesus.

In China myrrh was known as mooyao and was used medicinally from 600 AD during the Tang dynasty to treat wounds, relieve swelling and to treat menstrual pain. It is an antiseptic and was thought to help gum disease and bad breath.

Myrrh was a highly valued commodity that was traded along the spice routes. In the Middle East the Nabateans loaded it onto their camel caravans to transport it to their capital Petra, from where it was sent across to the Mediterranean. The Romans mixed myrrh with wine and gave it to prisoners before they were execcuted to relieve pain. Wealthy Romans would wear a pouch of myrrh around their necks as a perfume.

In Syriah the myrrh is named after the daughter of Thesis, a Syrian king who was transformed by the Gods into a myrrh tree to escape her father's wrath. Today the resin of the myrrh tree is a widely used fragrance in cosmetics, perfumes and soaps, as well as a flavouring. It is used as an astringent, as an antiseptic to be applied to inflamed lesions of the throat and mouth, as an antispasmodic, and for the treatment of infectious diseases. Myrrh also has a potential role in the treatment of schistosomiasis and fascioliasis; however, there is limited clinical information to support these uses.

'Myrrh tree', ink drawing by Joshua Swinton, 1911,
from a collection in *The British Library*.

NEEM

THE NEEM TREE has been revered in India for over two millennia, where it has been used in Ayurvedic medicine for over four thousand years and is said to have so many healing properties it has become known as a village pharmacy. Yet in many areas, including Sub-Saharan West Africa, and Australia, the neem is considered a weed.

Neem trees, or *Acadirachta indica*, actually belong to the family Meliaceae. They are tropical and sub-tropical trees, noted for their ability to resist drought. They are fast-growing, reaching a height of on average fifteen to twenty metres. Their branches are wide and spreading and they bear white, fragrant flowers and smooth, olive-like fruit. In India neem is thought to purify the atmosphere and kill germs. Therefore, it is grown at the south side of houses and in hospital grounds. Delivery rooms are fumigated with its burning bark. It is believed to be particularly protective of women and children.

Neem is a Hindi name, derived from the Sanscrit *nimba* from *nimbati systhyamdadati*, meaning 'to give good health'. The English name for neem is Margosa and its botanical name is *Azadirachta indica*. It is from the meliacae family and in Sanskrit it is called nimba. There are two types of neem – mittha or sweet neem, and karwa or bitter neem. There is a saying in Hindi, *Satya neem ki taraha karwaa hota hai:* 'The truth is as bitter as neem'.

Neem has been identified on 5000-year-old seals excavated from the Indus Valley civilization. The Vedas, the oldest Hindu scripts, detail the neem and its uses. So precious is the tree in the culture that in Andrah Pradesh the tree is known as *vepa*, or 'purifier of air'. It is also referred to as *arista*, which means 'perfect and everlasting, the reliever of sickness'. Elsewhere it is known as *pinchumada*, 'destroyer of leprosy' and Unani scholars refer to it as *shajar-e munalak*,' 'the blessed tree'. Indeed, neem's curative properties are believed by many to be of divine origin. Legend has it that a few drops of Amrita, the elixir of immortality, were dropped onto the Neem tree by Garmuda, a creature part-human, part-bird. Some believed that Sithala, the goddess of smallpox, lived in the branches of the neem and that the disease could be preented and cured by eating the leaves. Another myth holds that the Sun god Surya sought refuge from demons in a neem tree. To this day, Hindus believe that anyone who plants three neem trees is granted access after death to the kingdom of the sun, Suryalok, for three epochs.

Hinduism is not the only religion to value the neem. In Theravada Buddhism Tissa, the twentieth reincarnation of Buddha, is believed to have achieved enlightenment sitting beneath a neem, although some sources dispute this.

Ttoday neem oil continues to be the most widely used, commercially available product of the tree, a one-stop shop of healing, said to be antigungal, antibacterial, antiviral and contraceptive. In particular it is used to heal skin conditions, improve liver function and to detoxify and balance blood levels. It is equally popular as a mosquito repellent and as an insecticide in organic farming.

NUTMEG

NUTMEG, THE RARE, heady spice redolent of Christmas, is the seed kernel of the fruit of the nutmeg tree, of *Myristica fragrans*, literally 'myrrh-like fragrance'. The fruit is a drupe, about the size of an apricot which when ripe splits to reveal a single oval hard ball, wrapped by a delicate crimson thread that we know as mace.

For centuries the small archipelago of islands known as the Banda in Western Melanesia, nowadays known as the Spice islands, were the only place these beautiful tropical evergreens were grown. The Malays believed that nutmeg trees would not bear fruit unless they could grow near the sea and that they had to be fed with animal food.

Nutmeg trees can live for up to a hundred years and can yield up to 20,000 nutmegs a season, although this apparent abundance has never affected their spectacularly high price. In the Middle Ages it was reported that a pound of nutmeg cost as much as 'seven fat oxen'.

Nutmeg was traded in early history as a scent, an aphrodisiac and a medicine. The Romans called nutmeg *nux moschara*, literally 'musk nut', which was later to become *muscade nois* or 'perfumed nut' in old French. By the 6th century it had been transported along the great trade routes running from East to West, over 12,000 kilometres away from the islands where it had been harvested. In 1000 AD Abicenna described what he called the 'Banda nut'. It was used in traditional Indian medicine to soothe digestive and nervous complaints, as well as an aid to relieve muscular and rheumatic pain. In China it was known as *rou dou kou*.

Nutmeg was discovered when Antonio Pigafetta travelled to the islands on the HMS Victoria under the captainship of Ferdinand Magellan in 1520. Pigafetta wrote of a tree with a fruit like a quince apple. In the early 1600s, all but one of the islands, Pulo Run, were acquired by Dutch East India Company, enslaving the inhabitants, banning the export of the trees, and soaking them in lime to make them infertile. Stealing, growing and selling nutmeg trees was a crime punishable by death.

Pulo Run was taken over by the English and fiercely fought the Dutch for supremacy of their nutmeg. In a striking deal, Pulo Run was exchanged for a little known island called Manhattan. Nutmeg made the Dutch East India Company the richest corporation in the world. It would be 1769 before their dominance of the nutmeg market was broken, by an appropriately named Frenchman, Pierre Poivre. Poivre successfully smuggled nutmeg trees out of the country. Soon nutmeg trees were growing on Mauritius and in 1796 the islands fell back to the British, enabling nutmeg trees to be grown in Penang and Singapore.

The colourful history of the nutmeg tree and its precious seeds bears little resemblance to the small jars of nutmeg that we find on our supermarket shelves today. Nutmegs flavour culinary dishes, and their popularity as a traditional medicine has not waned. They are an excellent source of minerals, B-complex vitamins and many flavonoid anti-oxidants.

'Myristica fragrans', botanical drawing, 1901.

Banda Neira, one of the famous spice islands, in 1724.

OAK

THE ANCIENT OAK holds a special place in our hearts. Its resilience and fortitude have made it renowned as the king of the forest. Some even say that England was built on oak and indeed, the tree has been here for much longer than humanity. Fossils date back to the interglacial period 300,000 years ago when remains suggest people made bread from oak acorns.

For centuries The Christmas Yule log was e a real oak log decorated with holly. People put acorns in their pockets to bring good luck and prosperity. And it was customary for young people spoke their wedding vows beneath a spreading oak.

An iconic symbol of strength, the Greeks and Romans held that the oak was a magical tree. Roman guards wove oak leaf bands around their heads to show courage and victory. Herodotus wrote in the mid 400s BC that oak trees were believed to have the gift of prophecy. Greek soldiers used Q. *coccifera*, as a dye. A scarlet stain produced from the wood was from the galls made by female wasps laying eggs in the bark. Spartans used the dye in their battle garments or mixed it with iron to make ink.

In Greek mythology the oak tree was the sacred tree of the God Zeus. In Slavic and Baltic tradition it was the holy tree of Perun, god of thunder; and the Norse thunder God Thor held the oak sacred. In the Bible Isaiah referred to the Israelites as 'oaks of righteousness'.

Oaks belong to the genus Quercus and divide into around 600 different species, including both deciduous and evergreen and range from preferring cool temperate climates to tropical. Around 90 species are to be found in the Americas and 160 in Mexico. China has around 100. Oaks support more wildlife than any other tree, including 280 kinds of insect. Bats roost in old woodpecker holes in their trunks and mistletoe lives on oak branches. Their wood has been used to build homes, furniture and ships for many centuries. The trees are intertwined with our history. After the battle of Worcester in 1651 King Charles II hid from the Roundheads in a large oak at Boscobel. In 1660 he instigated the 29th of May as Royal Oak Day to celebrate the restoration of the monarchy. The River Severn's ancient oak breakwaters are still in use, put in by Romans.

Many parishes used to contain a Gospel Oak, a great tree at which part of the Gospel was read out during the Beating of the Bounds ceremonies at Rogantide. In Somerset the two oaks of Gog and Magog, named after the last male and female giants to roam Britain, are said to be the remnants of an oak-lined processional route up to the nearby Glastonbury Tor. Legend has it the Major Oak in Sherwood Forest is the tree where Robin Hood and his Merry Men hatched their plots. The Topless Oaks in Bradgate Park are said to have been pollarded as a sign of mourning following the beheading, in 1554, of Lady Jane Grey. The largest recorded English oak was the Newlands oak, which measured 45 feet around the base of the trunk. Today the oldest tree, the Bowthorpe Oak, lies in Lincolnshire. It is hollow, with a girth of 33 feet and has room for twenty people to stand inside. It is estimated to be almost 1000 years old.

'Gigantic oak tree on the Tejon Ranch, Kern county', 1910,
Library of Congress.

OLIVE

OLives, or *Olea europaea*, are the oldest fruit trees and certainly are one of the most important ones in history. Olive tree culture has been closely connected to the rise and fall of Mediterranean empires and other advanced civilizations throughout the ages. Olive wood fragments and pits have been discovered in Early Bronze Age tombs. In ancient Egypt olives were a symbol of prosperity, purity and blessing, mentioned in the Hebrew Bible and with just as important a role in the Christian Old Testament where it is written that a dove brought Noah an olive branch as a sign that the waters had receded.

Fossilized leaves of the olive were discovered on the Greek island of Santorini dating back to 60,000 BP, the oldest known olives in the Mediterranean and as far back as 3000 BC olives were cultivated and traded in Crete. Burnt at temples, in ancient Greece olive oil was used to anoint kings and used to light the flame of the games at Olympus. Those who triumphed wore crowns of olive leaves.

In Rome olive trees were widespread and Romans spread olive oil onto their skin to moisturize it. According to Pliny the Elder a vine, a fig tree and an olive tree grew in the centre of the Roman Forum. In mythology the hero Hercules is reported to have killed the terrifying Lion of Cithaeron with his own hands using a wooden stake made from an olive tree. In several of his Twelve Labors, Hercules also used clubs made of olive wood to corner an enemy. Once cornered, he would then strangle or kill the enemy with his bare hands. Because these stories were so popular, the olive tree became associated with strength, resistance and power.

Another myth tells how Theseus, son of an Athenian king, was sent as a part of a yearly human sacrifice to Knossos on Crete to be fed into a gigantic labyrinth and killed by the dreaded Minotaur. Prior to leaving, Theseus begged Apollo for protection and was given a sacred olive branch from the Acropolis of Athens. Theseus killed the Minotaur and according to one myth, was able to escape from the labyrinth because of a string he had tied around an olive branch.

The Arabs brought olives to Spain along with their new religion, spread through trade and battle from the seventh century. The Qur'an praised the olive as a precious fruit. The Qur'an states that 'Allah is the Light of the Heavens and Earth. The similitude of His light is a niche wherein is a lamp... kindled from a blessed tree, an olive.' Elsewhere, the Prophet Muhammad is reported to have said, 'Take oil of the olive and massage with it – it is a blessed tree.'

The olive tree is an international symbol and to this day the flag of the United Nations bears a branch as a message of harmony and peace between countries.

'An aged olive tree in Gethsemane', ink drawing c.1953,
The British Library.

ORANGE

ORANGES TREES, *CITRUS sinesis* or *Citrus aurantium*, include blood and naval, sweet and bitter oranges, which featured in the literature of China as long ago as 314 BC. It is thought that they originated in the region as long ago as 2500 BC.

Many believe that the orange is the 'golden apple' spoken of in Greek mythology. The golden apple was the fruit that Juno gave to Jupiter on the day of their celestial wedding.

Invading Muslims during the early spread of Islam took oranges to the country then named Al-Andalus, or Andalucia, in the 8th and 9th centuries. By the 10th century their cultivation in the region was widespread and just over a century later their fruit was being eaten and used as medicine in Italy.

The sweet orange was relatively unknown in the less temperate climates of Northern Europe. Italian and Portuguese sailors transported the trees to Britain during the 15th century where it became known as an exotic, a preserve of the rich grown in orangeries to fend off the frost.

Although scurvy had not yet been discovered, during the Age of Discovery sailors would plant orange trees along their trade routes believing them to be beneficial to good health. Christopher Columbus may have planted the trees on his second voyage to Hispaniola in 1495 and further expeditions took the orange further afield to the Americas; and in 1565 the Spanish seaman and adventurer Pedro Menéndes de Avilés founded St Augustine and his missionaries carried the orange tree to Arizona. A century later Fransiscan monks were also planting oranges in San Diego.

Orange trees were planted on the Hawaiian islands thanks to the botanist and naturalist Archibald Menzies, who collected their seeds in South Africa on the Vancouver expedition, a four and a half voyage of exploration and diplomacy commanded by Captain George Vancouver. Menzies raised the seedling trees on board and gave them as gifts to Hawaiian chiefs in 1982. Unfortunately, however, many of the trees in Hawaii were subsequently wiped out with the arrival of fruit fly in the early nineteenth century.

In many cultures oranges are the symbol of love and marriage, fertility and purity. Traditionally, an orange featured in a painting denoted marital harmony and prosperity, such as in Jan van Eyck's Wedding *Portrait of the Arnolfini*. The exchange of an orange between unmarried men and women was a simple charm to invite love to blossom between the two. In the legend of Nell Gwynn, the orange seller who won the heart of the English King, the orange is a symbol of seduction.

Queen Victoria was given a coronet of gold and enamel orange blossoms by Prince Albert. When their children were born he instructed a jeweler to add a small fruit to the piece. Their leaves were used to make tea and their wood to season meat. To this day orange blossom is a base note in many cosmetics and perfumes.

PEACH

ALTHOUGH THE PEACH tree's botanical name *Prunus persica* refers to Persia from where it came to Europe, genetic studies suggest peaches originated in China where they have been cultivated since the early days of Chinese culture since 2000 BC. Peaches were mentioned in Chinese writings as far back as the 10th century BC and were eaten by of kings and emperors. The ancient Chinese believed the peach to possess more vitality than any other tree because their blossoms appear before leaves sprout. When early rulers of China visited their territories, sorcerers accompanied them, armed with peach rods to protect them from spectral evils. On New Year's Eve, local magistrates would cut peach wood branches and place them over their doors to protect against evil influences.

The Chinese also considered peach wood (*t'ao-fu*) protective against evil spirits, who held the peach in awe. In ancient China, peach-wood bows were used to shoot arrows in every direction in an effort to dispel evil. Peach-wood slips or carved pits served as amulets to protect a person's life, safety, and health. Peach-wood seals or figurines guarded gates and doors, and, as one Han account recites, 'the buildings in the capital are made tranquil and pure; everywhere a good state of affairs prevails'.

The peach was brought to India and Western Asia in ancient times. Peach cultivation reached Greece by 300 BC. Alexander the Great introduced the fruit into Europe after he conquered the Persians. Peaches were also well known to the Romans in first century AD and were cultivated widely in Emilia-Romagna. Peach trees are portrayed in the wall paintings of the towns destroyed by the Vesuvius eruption of 79 AD, while the oldest known representations of the fruit are in two fragments of wall paintings from the first century AD, now preserved in the National Archaeological Museum in Naples.

The peach was brought to the Americas by Spanish explorers in the sixteenth century, and eventually to England and France in the seventeenth century, where it was an expensive treat. The horticulturist George Minifie brought peaches from England to North America in the early seventeenth century, planting them at his estate in Virginia. Thomas Jefferson had peach trees at Monticello, but farmers did not begin cultivation until the nineteenth century.

Many famous artists have painted still life with peach fruits placed in prominence. Caravaggio, Vicenzo Campi, Pierre-Auguste Renoir, Claude Monet, Édouard Manet, Henri Jean Fantin-Latour, Peter Paul Rubens, Van Gogh are among the many influential artists who painted peaches and peach trees in various settings. Scholars suggest that many compositions are symbolic, some an effort to introduce realism. The artists of Renaissance symbolically used peach to represent the heart, and a leaf attached to the fruit as the symbol for tongue, thereby implying speaking truth from one's heart; a ripe peach was a symbol to imply a ripe state of good health. Caravaggio paintings introduce realism by painting peach leaves that are molted, discolored or in some cases have wormholes – conditions common in modern peach cultivation.

'Peach tree branches with leaves and blossoms', by Henry Turnball, 1811.

PEAR

PEAR CULTIVATION IN cool temperate climates extends to the remotest antiquity, and there is evidence of its use as a food since prehistoric times. Many traces of it have been found in prehistoric pile dwellings around Lake Zurich. The word 'pear', or its equivalent, occurs in all the Celtic languages.

The pear was widely cultivated in ancient times by both the Greeks and Romans, who ate the fruits raw or cooked, just like apples. Pliny's *Natural History* recommended stewing them with honey and noted three dozen varieties. The Roman cookbook *De re coquinaria* has a recipe for a spiced, stewed-pear *patina*, or soufflé. Pears were considered an aphrodisiac and the fruit was consecrated to Aphrodite and Venus, the goddesses of love.

By the thirteenth century many varieties of pears had been imported from France and the fruit was used mainly for cooking rather than eating raw. Court accounts of Henry III of England record pears shipped from La Rochelle-Normande and presented to the King by the Sheriffs of the City of London. A hundred years on the Warden pear had been bred and became famous for its use in pies. The variety is mentioned in Shakespeare's *The Winter's Tale*. By 1640, at least 64 varieties were being cultivated in England and at about this time grafting onto quince rootstock began to replace pear and crab apples rootstocks. In the 18th century new and improved strains were introduced from what is now Belgium. However, the majority of pears continued to be used for cooking. Dessert pears were grown mainly in private gardens but were unsuitable for commercial cultivation. One exception was the William's Pear, raised in about 1770 by a schoolmaster in Aldermaston in Berkshire, which became very popular and is still produced on a limited scale today. Another old variety, the Worcester, has the distinction of figuring in the coat-of-arms of the city of Worcester, although this large deep russeted culinary pear has virtually disappeared.

Pears have been cultivated in China for approximately 3000 years. The genus is thought to have originated in present-day Western China in the foothills of the Tian Shan, a mountain range of Central Asia, and to have spread to the north and south along mountain chains, evolving into a diverse group of over 20 widely recognized primary species.

Early in the nineteenth century Thomas Andrew Knight began to develop new pear varieties. The Royal Horticultural Society encouraged pear growing and in 1826 there were 622 varieties in their gardens at Chiswick. A breakthrough in dessert varieties took place in 1858 with the introduction into England of the Doyenne du Comice, commonly known as Comice. But the first significant English pear to be produced by controlled breeding was Fertility in 1875, although this variety is no longer produced commercially. Conference was introduced in 1894 and along with Comice soon overshadowed all other varieties. In the later half of the twentieth century, Conference took over in popularity and today represents more than 90% of commercial production in Britain.

'Three trees undergoing plant physiology experiments, including
demonstration that suction of roots can overcome the force of gravity',
1810, *The British Library.*

PINE

THE PINE FAMILY includes pines, larches and spruces, from which, among other things, paper is made, the hemlocks, the tannin in whose bark helps make leather, the firs, cypresses, sequoias, cedars and junipers. They are all commonly referred to as evergreens because, with the exception of the larch and the bald cypress, their leaves do not fall all at once as do those of most trees.

Pine trees have been a key factor in the advancement of mankind. It is believed by some that early caveman evolved into the neanderthal when he learned how to build with pine. The evolving men would drive posts into the ground and strap pine tree limbs to the top using the sinews of animals. Resin from the pine tree was used to help secure pine tree needles to the roof for shelter. The men would collect pine cones from the forests of towering pine trees and place them on the smoldering embers of their fires and the resin would act with the moisture of the pine cones and burn for hours. The men would also catch fish with triton's made from twisted and carved pine tree branches, and kill boar, and small game with spears caved from the small, strait, trunks of young pine trees. As their women folk would make loin cloths from the skins of large animals and cook food over flames, men began to experiment with building shelters from the wood.

In mythology pines are frequently associated with dwelling

places of fairies and gnomes, and thought of as benevolent, refreshing places where tired walkers can safely rest in the protective aura of the tree. They symbolize humbleness, good fortune and prosperity , fertility and protection. Their needles stay green even through the harsh winter months, and thus their evergreen nature has been interpreted as a sign of their vitality. In the past, farmers sought to transfer this vital force and its protective powers to their barns and stables by sweeping the floors with brushes wound from pine twigs and pinning some above doors. The needles were thought to ward off witchcraft and protect house and cattle from misfortune, disease and even lightning. In Germany, as the foundations of a new building are laid, the raw structure is sometimes still crowned with a decorated pine tree, to attract protection and prosperity.

Pine trees are evergreen, coniferous trees that are found in almost all parts of the world. There are approximately one hundred twenty species of pine trees. There are short pine trees, tall pine trees, wide pine trees, skinny pine trees and coloured Pine trees. Pine trees have green to bluish grey leaves in the form of needles that are arranged in bundles of two to five or six to eight, depending on species. Pine trees are also known as survival plants. The cambium, or sub-bark, is moist and almost sweet, but rich in vitamins A and C. In Sweden in the winter the Swedes often make 'strunt' tea from the needles and tiny baby pine cones of the *Pinus nigra* – the European Black Pine tree or Austrian Pine.

Pines are also extremely adaptable, so much so that they are known to naturally cross-pollinate between species to evolve into an improved species. This is the case with the Sonderegger Pine, *Pinus palastris*, *Pinus teada*, of the Southeast. A natural hybrid cross between Longleaf Pine and Loblolly pine that takes on the best qualities of both species: longer pine needles and fatter pine cones with faster consistent growth, resulting in a mature tree in an unbelievably short amount of time.

Pine is the leading source of paper products and building materials in the world. Loblolly pine, *Pinus teada*, is one of the leading timber species in America, growing from New Jersey to Florida to Texas. The timbers of this species are very compact and make them a great choice for pine tree flooring.

In the nineteenth century, pine growers noticed that the sap from pine trees could be collected and boiled down with several bi-products that could be equally marketed, making the tree sap Boom so successful. Resin oil could be taken for cough, and scratchy throat, and some soaps, and glues were also processed, with turpentine as the primary bi-product. Pine trees also began to be harvested around this time, devastating forests to make paper, and build houses.

Nowadays pines are among the most commercially important tree species in the world, valued for their timber and wood pulp. They are fast-growing softwoods that will grow in relatively dense stands, their acidic decaying needles inhibiting the sprouting of competing hardwoods. Commercial pines are grown in plantations for timber that is denser, more resinous, and therefore more durable than spruce. The wood is widely used in high-value carpentry items such as furniture, window frames, panelling, floors and roofing, and the resin of some species is an important source of turpentine.

'Preparing Christmas greens and making wreaths', 1876, *Library of Congress.*

POMEGRANATE

P OMEGRANATES HAVE BEEN cultivated throughout the Middle East, South Asia, and Mediterranean region for several millennia, and also thrive in the drier climates of California and Arizona. The pomegranate tree is also extensively grown in South China and in Southeast Asia and Kandahar is famous in Afghanistan for its high-quality pomegranates. Berber women used pomegranates to predict the number of their offspring by drawing a circle on the ground and dropping a ripe pomegranate in the centre The number of seeds outside the ring allegedly predicts the number of future children. Although not native to Korea or Japan, the pomegranate is widely grown there and many cultivars have been developed. It is widely used for bonsai because of its flowers and for the unusual twisted bark the older specimens can attain.

Evidence of the fruit has been identified in early Bronze Age levels Jericho in the West Bank, as well as late Bronze Age levels of Hala Sultan Tekke on Cyprus and Tiryns. A large, dry pomegranate was found in the tomb of Djehuty, the butler of Queen Hatshepsut in Egypt; Mesopotamian cuneiform records mention pomegranate trees and their fruit from the mid-third millennium BC onwards. Legends of the pomegranate also abound in Greek myth. Perhaps its most famous is that of Persephone, a beautiful maiden desired by Hades, who decided that she would be his wife and companion in the dark world of the dead. To this end, he kidnapped her and brought her to live with him for eternity in the underworld. Persephone's mother, Demeter, the goddess of the harvest, was so distraught that she caused every plant on Earth to die. To avoid a catastrophic loss of all life, Zeus commanded Hades to allow Persephone to return to her home. However, before she was able return, Hades tricked her into eating four seeds from the pomegranate, an action that condemned her to life in the underworld for four months out of every year.

Symbol of fertility, eternal life and renewal, in Buddhist legend, a demon-woman was cured of her love of eating children through the deep red juices of the pomegranate. In ancient Persia, the pomegranate was believed to bring invincibility to battle. Spears would be balanced with weighted silver and gold sculptures of ripe pomegranates. And to the early Hebrews, the pomegranate's seeds were an affirmation of their faith. Each pomegranate was believed to contain exactly 613 seeds, a number that corresponds with the number of commandments in the Torah. This belief was once so strong that the Old Testament directs for the pomegranate's image to be woven into priestly robes.

Indeed some Biblical scholars argue that the pomegranate was also the original fruit from the Garden of Eden, making it the representation of all that is forbidden. One taste of its ripe seeds and all knowledge of death, sex, and sin are suddenly clear. This didn't stop early Christians from venerating the fruit. Christian iconic paintings often depict the Virgin Mary with a pomegranate either in her hand or nearby. In this way, it was used to demonstrate the Virgin Mary's power over life and death, as well as the seed that bore the son of God.

The pomegranate was introduced as an exotic to England by John Tradescant the elder, but the disappointment that it did not set fruit there led to its repeated introduction to the American colonies, even New England. It succeeded in the South: Bartram received a barrel of pomegranates and oranges from a correspondent in Charleston, South Carolina, 1764. John Bartram partook of pomegranates with Noble Jones at Wormsloe Plantation, near Savannah, Georgia, in September 1765. Thomas Jefferson planted pomegranates at Monticello in 1771: he had them from George Wythe of Williamsburg. The ancient city of Granada in Spain was renamed after the fruit during the Moorish period. Still today the province of Granada uses pomegranate as a charge in heraldry for its canting arms.

Spanish colonists later introduced pomegranate trees and their fruit to the Caribbean and South America but in the English colonies, the pomegranate tree proved to be less at home: 'Don't use the pomegranate inhospitably, a stranger that has come so far to pay his respects to thee,' the English Quaker Peter Collinson wrote to the botanizing John Bartram in Philadelphia, 1762. Shortly afterwards, the celebrated English physician, Quaker and plant hunter Dr Fothergill commented, 'Plant it against the side of thy house, nail it close to the wall. In this manner it thrives wonderfully with us, and flowers beautifully, and bears fruit this hot year. I have twenty-four on one tree, but of all trees this is most salutiferous to mankind.' It might be argued that these words of praise ring just as true today as they did then.

POPLAR

O VID, WHO WROTE 'So falls a poplar that on watery ground, raised high its head with stately branches crowned.' held that Paris carved the name of Ænone on a poplar, as Shakespeare has Orlando carve the name of Rosalind upon the trees of the forest of Arden. Virgil gives directions for the culture of this tree and Horace speaks of the White Poplar as delighting to grow on the banks of rivers.

Ancient Greek and Roman mythology abounds with other stories about the elegant poplar. It was said that the White Poplar was consecrated to Hercules when he destroyed Cacus in a cavern adjoining the Aventine Hill, which was covered with poplar trees; and in the moment of his triumph he bound his brows with a branch of White Poplar as a token of his victory. Anyone offering sacrifices to Hercules was always crowned with branches of poplar; and all who had gloriously conquered their enemies in battle wore garlands of it, in imitation of Hercules. Homer in the Iliad compares the fall of Simoisius when killed by Ajax to that of a poplar.

It was also a widely held belief that the nymph Leuce was metamorphosed into a white poplar by Persephone to save her from being raped by Hades. According to another myth, Hades planted an aspen tree in the Elysian Fields to honor his mistress, the nymph Leuce. White poplar was associated with Leuce, leprosy. A leper colony in ancient Greece was under the protection of Zeus of the white poplar. Lepreans worshipped the white poplar. The moon goddess of the white poplar cured skin disease.

Poplar wood was also considered an antidote to a serpent's bite. It was dedicated to Alcides Hercules as a god of healing powers. Zeus killed Phaëthon with a thunderbolt because he was unable to control the sun chariot he had stolen from his father Helios. The Heliads, his grieving sisters, were metamorphosed into weeping poplar trees whose tears turned to amber as they fell into a stream.

In Celtic mythology the poplar is associated with victory, transformation and vision and is referred to as the talking, whispering and quivering tree. It is said to have the ability to endure and conquer. Heracles wore a crown of poplar leaves when he retrieved Cerberus from Hades. The upper surface of the leaves was thus darkened from Hades' fumes.

Poplars have a very strong set of roots, which affords them the symbolic value of grounding, security and strength. They're also require very little care, if any. No wonder that even back in 1841 the American landscape designer and horticulturalist Andrew Jackson Downing wrote of these tall, elegant trees that they give 'life, spirit and variety to any scene composed entirely of round-headed trees'.

'Lombardy poplar trees, Longacres, Southwest Sixteenth Street, Renton, King County', *Library of Congress*.

QUINCE

T HE QUINCE, OR *Cydonia oblonga*, is the sole member of the genus in the family Rosaceae (which also contains apples and pears, among other fruits). It is a small deciduous tree that bears a pome fruit, similar in appearance to a pear, bright golden-yellow when mature, and a native of Persia, Anatolia, Greece and the Crimea. It is certain that the ancient Greeks knew a common variety, upon which they grafted scions of a better variety, which they obtained from Cydon in Crete, from which place the fruit derived its name of cydonia, of which the English name Quince is a corruption. The fruit was known to the Akkadians in ancient Mesopotamia, who called it *supurgillu*; Arabic *al safarjal*, or 'quinces'.

In Classical times the Quince was held sacred to Venus, who is often depicted with a Quince in her right hand, the gift she received from Paris. The 'golden Apples' of Virgil are said to be Quinces, as they were the only 'golden' fruit known in his time, oranges having only been introduced into Italy at the time of the Crusades. Symbol of love and happiness, Plutarch mentions the bridal custom of a quince being shared by a married pair. Quinces sent as presents, or shared, were tokens of love. The custom survived, and throughout the Middle Ages Quinces were used at every wedding feast, listed among recipes relating to domestic life in England. Wynkyn de Worde, in the *Boke of Kervynge*, wrote of 'char de Quynce,' and John Russell, in the *Boke of Nurture*, of 'chare de Quynces', the old name for Quince Marmalade. The modern name originated in the fourteenth century as a plural of *quoyn*, via Old French *cooin* from Latin *cydonium malum*, derived originally from the Greek *kydonion melon*.

In Carolina in 1709, John Lawson allowed that he was 'not a fair judge of the different sorts of Quinces, which they call Brunswick, Portugal and Barbary', but he noted 'of this fruit they make a wine or liquor which they call Quince-Drink, and which I approve of beyond any that their country affords, though a great deal of cider and perry is there made, The Quince-Drink most commonly purges'.

Quince is known to be a bitter, hard fruit, but some varieties of quince, such as 'Aromatnaya' and 'Kuganskaya' do not require cooking and can be eaten raw. However, most varieties of quince are too sour to eat raw unless bletted (softened by frost and subsequent decay). High in pectin, they are used to make jam, jelly and quince pudding, or they may be peeled, then roasted, baked or stewed; pectin levels diminish as the fruit ripens. The flesh of the fruit turns red after a long cooking time and the strong perfume means they can be added in small quantities to apple pies and jam to enhance the flavor. Adding a diced quince to apple sauce will enhance the taste of the apple sauce with the chunks of relatively firm, tart quince. In Kashmir, India, quinces are harvested for their 'Bum-choonth', cooked with brinjals and enjoyed as a delicacy. In the Balkans and elsewhere, quince brandy, marmalade and liqueur are as popular today as ever.

ROWAN

The European rowan (*Sorbus aucuparia*) has a long tradition in European mythology and folklore. It was thought to give protection against malevolent beings. The tree was also called 'wayfarer's tree' or 'traveller's tree' because it supposedly prevents those on a journey from getting lost. It was said in England that this was the tree on which the Devil hanged his mother.

British folklorists of the Victorian era reported the belief in apotropaic powers of the rowan-tree, in particular in the warding off of witches. Such a report is given by Edwin Lees (1856) for the Wyre Forest in the English West Midlands. Sir James Frazer (1890) reported such a tradition in Scotland, where the tree was often planted near a gate or front door. According to Frazer, birds' droppings often contain rowan seeds, and if such droppings land in a fork or hole where old leaves have accumulated on a larger tree, such as an oak or a maple, they may result in a 'flying' rowan growing as an epiphyte on the larger tree, thought of as especially potent against witches and sorcery.

In 1891, the American folklorist, humororist and writer Charles Godfrey Leland also wrote of the rowan's apparent apotropaic powers against witches in English cultural traditions, citing the *Denham Tracts* the old English name of the rowan, *cwic-beám*, a reference which survives in the name quickbeam, quicken or quicken-tree. This name by the nineteenth century was reinterpreted as connected to the word witch, from a dialectal variant wick for quick and names such as wicken-tree, wich-tree, wicky, wiggan-tree, giving rise to witch-hazel and witch-tree.

In Norse mythology, the goddess Sif is the wife of the thunder god Thor. Sif has been linked with Ravdna, the consort of the Sami thunder-god Horagalles. Red berries of rowan were holy to Ravdna, and the name *Ravdna* resembles North Germanic words for the tree (for example, Old Norse *reynir*). According to *Skáldskaparmál* the rowan is called 'the salvation of Thor' because Thor once saved himself by clinging to it. The Celts held that the Rowan is a 'portal tree', the threshold, between this world and the next. Hence, during the Middle Ages it was often planted at the gate to a property, signifying the crossing of the threshold between the path or street and the property of someone.

In North America popular myth has it that a heavy crop of rowan fruit means a hard or difficult winter, while in Scandinavia and, in particular, Sweden, the number of fruit on the trees was used as a predictor of the snow cover during winter. It was also thought that if the rowan trees grew pale and lost colour, the autumn and winter would bring much illness. The Finnish Sipoo people determined that winter had begun when the waxwings (*Bombycilla garrulus*) had eaten the last of the rowan fruit. They believed the reverse. If the rowan flowers were plentiful then the rye harvest would also be plentiful. Similarly, if the rowan flowered twice in a year there would be many potatoes and many weddings that autumn.

SANDALWOOD

AN ANCIENT BUDDHIST scripture states: 'None but the Mali Mountains contain sandalwood. One of the oldest incense materials, sandalwood has been in use for at least 4,000 years. It is one of the most calming incenses and therefore is one of the preferred ones for meditation. It is believed to calm the mind, enhance mental clarity, and to aid in the opening of the Third Eye. Many ancient temples, rosaries and staffs are made from sandalwood.

The sandal tree, or *Santalum album*, belongs to the family Santalaceae. The tree grows almost exclusively in the forests of Karnataka, followed by Tamil Nadu, Kerala and Andhra Pradesh, Timor Islands of Indonesia. As the tree grows, the essential oil develops in the roots and heartwood, which requires at least 15 to 20 years. Full maturity is reached after 60 to 80 years. The core of dark heartwood gradually develops, which is covered by outer sapwood.

A sandalwood tree is never felled, but uprooted in the rainy season, when the roots are richer in the precious essential oil. Vietnam and New Caledonia have long controlled plantations of genuine sandalwood. The best quality oil comes from the Indian provinces of Mysore and Tamil Nadu, where the harvest of trees are protected by the government. The tree is medium sized 12-15 meters tall. The tree reaches its full maturity in 60 to 80 years, which is when the center of the slender trunk (the heart wood) has achieved its greatest oil content.

Both the heartwood and roots are fragrant and contain the oil; the bark and sapwood however are odorless. The Sandalwood tree is never cut down, but uprooted during rainy season, when it is richer in precious essential oils. The sandal tree does very well on its own, and seems to appear in places it was never seen before. However all attempts by man to proliferate and increase the growth of the species have yielded declining plant populations.

Many people feel that no essential oil produced from any Sandalwood tree (even Mysore) has the same psychotropic, emotional, spiritual, or medicinal benefits that we find in the wood powder or incense burning that is centuries old. Ayurvedic healers either used powdered Sandalwood or the burning of Sandalwood in their ancient practice. Essential oils and attars may have also been used in Indian medicine, but were popularized in the west by the perfume industry and so became applied medicinally in the western world after the 1920's by French aromatherapists.

Pterocarpus santalius or santalum rubrum, or red sandalwood, are used for colouring and dyeing. Other varieties come from the Sandwich islands, Western Australia and New Caledonia. The Australian *S. spicatum* or *Eucarya spicata* produces a very similar oil but with a dry-bitter top note.

Sandalwood is mentioned in Sanskrit and Chinese manuscripts dating back 4000 years. The oil was used in religious ritual, and many deities and temples were carved from its wood. The wood is soft to carve and is frequently used in sacred fragrant carvings. The ancient Egyptians imported the wood and used it in medicine, embalming and ritual burning to venerate their gods. In Buddhism, it is considered to be one of the three incenses integral to Buddhist practice, together with

Aloes wood and Cloves. Depression, anxiety and insomnia were treated with sandalwood. It was believed to promote spiritual practices, peaceful relaxation and openness. It is used in many death ceremonies to help the crossing over, and to comfort mourners.

Sandalwood oil has been widely used in folk medicine for treatment of common colds, bronchitis, skin disorders, heart ailments, general weakness, fever, infection of the urinary tract, inflammation of the mouth and pharynx, liver and gallbladder complaints and other maladies. Recently, the *in vivo* anti-hyperglycemic and antioxidant potentials of α-santalol and sandalwood oil were demonstrated in Swiss Albino mice. Additionally, different *in vitro* and *in vivo* parts of the plant have been shown to possess antimicrobial and antioxidant properties,*S. album* in India also features as a construction material in temples and elsewhere. The Indian government has banned the export of the species to reduce the threat by over-harvesting. In the southern Indian states of Karnataka and Andhra Pradesh all trees of greater than a specified girth are the property of the state. Felling of sandal trees, even on private property, is regulated by the government.

Sandalwood was an important early trade in nineteenth-century Australasia.

SPRUCE

THERE ARE THIRTY-five species of spruce trees, all belonging to the Pine family. Spruces, like firs, with which they share a great deal in common, prefer cooler climates. They are to be found widely in Northern Europe and North America where they can survive in high, mountainous regions with poor soil quality and are mythologically important plants among the native tribes, symbols of the sky and guardians. According to one myth, the spruce tree was once a medicine man, Salavi, who transformed himself into a tree. For this reason, spruce trees are considered particularly sacred to the Hopis, who use spruce boughs to adorn kachina dancers. Another tribal legend tells how the father and mother of the Pima people survived the deluge by floating in a ball of spruce pitch. Among northern tribes, spruce trees are associated with peace and protection. To the Salish tribes, the spruce has always been a symbol of good luck. The roots are used in basketry. Northern Algonquian tribes used to bundle spruce and fir needles into sachets or herbal pillows to protect against illness.

The name spruce originally entered the English language during the sixteenth century from the Polish for Prussia or 'Prusy'. The name was used to describe many goods imported to Great Britain from that part of the world. Spruce also meant dapper, referring to dandies who dressed in the latest fashions made from high quality materials originating from Prussia.

Spruces have a naturally high vitamin C content and in 1593

the French navigator Jacques Cartier chanced upon the medicinal benefits known for centuries by the native Indians. Cartier was exploring the shores along the St Lawrence River in present-day Ontario, Canada, when his seamen fell ill from scurvy and were saved by the native Iroquoian tribe who made a tea brewed from the needles of the spruce.

Cartier's seamen were saved and henceforth not only spruce tea but beer made of the tops and branches of the tree, boiled for hours, strained into casks and sweetened with molasses became a medical necessity for sailors bound on long seafaring journeys. During the eighteenth century exploration of the North American, Pacific and Australasian coasts most ships carried on board their own particular recipe for the brew. One, dating from 1796, advised: 'Take four ounces of hops, let them boil half an hour in one gallon of water, strain the hop water then add sixteen gallons of warm water, two gallons of molasses, eight ounces of essence of spruce, dissolved in one quart of water, put it in a clean cask, then shake it well together, add half a pint of emptins, then let it stand and work one week, if very warm weather less time will do, when it is drawn off to bottle, add one spoonful of molasses to every bottle.'

Nowadays, spruce has many diverse uses, from fences at Aintree racecourse to artistic sculptures. The wood is an essential building material and has even been employed in making aircraft. The Wright brothers' first flying machine, the Flyer, was made of spruce, as are many musical instrument soundboards due to its natural acoustic qualities.

Above: 'Great Alaskan spruces', lithograph circa 1920,
Library of Congress.

Left: the making of Spruce beer, 1875.

STRAWBERRY

Oh green Italian tree, your May month
is in the mist: if everything die,
you, the youthful wild banner
unfold to the northern wind

WHEN THE ITALIAN poet Giovanni Pascoli wrote lines of the strawberry tree he was hinting at a passage in the great Greek masterpiece, the Aeneid, in which Pallas, killed by Turnus, posed on branches of strawberry tree. Pascoli saw the colours of the tree a prefiguration of the flag of Italy and considered Pallas the first martyr. Indeed nowadays the tree makes up part of the Coat of arms of Madrid (*El oso y el madroño*, The Bear and the Strawberry Tree) of the city of Madrid, Spain and in the city centre stands a statue of a bear eating the fruit of the *Madroño* tree. The motif appears on crests, taxis and man-hole covers.

The strawberry tree, or *arbutus unedo*, was notable in Roman Italy, when Pliny thought it should not be planted where bees were kept, for the bitterness it imparted to honey. The tree was considered a sign of good luck and its flowers laid on the graves as a sign of respect for those who had passed away. Even today in some regions of southern Italy it is possible to find strawberry tree branches with three berries hung at home as a sign of prosperity. During the Italian Risorgimento the strawberry tree was considered a symbol of the national unity. The fact of bringing on its branches, at the same time, the green leaves, the white flowers and the red berries had uplifted the tree, in fact, as a symbol of the national tricolor flag.

The strawberry tree was also common elsewhere in the Mediterranean and Western Europe, including Ireland where it was known for centuries as the Irish strawberry or cane apple, from the Gaelic *caithne*. From Italy it was carried into northern European gardens and to England. In 1586 a correspondent in Ireland sent plants to the Elizabethan courtiers Lord Leicester and Sir Francis Walsingham and in 1649 Henrietta Maria described 'one very fayre tree, called the Irish arbutis standing in the midle parte of the sayd kitchin garden, very lovely to look upon'.

By the eighteenth century the strawberry tree was well known enough in English gardens for Batty Langley to make the bold and impractical suggestion that it might be used for hedges, though it 'will not admit of being clipped as other evergreens are'. In the United States of America Thomas Jefferson admiringly mentioned a strawberry tree growing in his Monticello gardens in 1778.

Although bitter to the taste and not recommended to be eaten raw, the fruit of the *Madroño* tree naturally ferments on the tree if left to ripen and is used to make several alcoholic beverages, and liqueurs such as the Portuguese *medronho*, a type of strong brandy. *Aguardente de Medronhos* is known as firewater to non-Portuguese speakers, and obtains this name from the hot sensation as the consumed beverage travels down the throat and is felt through the sinuses and since *água ardente* is portuguese for burning water. Albanians prepare another traditional fiery drink known as *raki* from the strawberry tree.

SYCAMORE

THE SYCAMORE IS rich in cultural and historical significance. As far back as 480BC Herodotus recorded a time that Xerxes was traveling through Lydia in which he found a tree so beautifulthat he presented it with golden ornaments, and put it under the care of one of his Immortals. In the Bible the tax collector Zaccheus stood beneath a sycamore tree so that he could see Jesus. And in Egyptian mythology the sycamore tree was thought to be the embodiment of three goddesses: Isis, Nut and Hathor, the Lady of the Sycamore.

The common name sycamore originally applied to the fig *Ficus sycomorus*, the sycamore or sycamore referred to in the Bible that is native to southwest Asia. Other common names for the tree include false plane-tree great maple, Scottish maple, mount maple, mock-plane, or Celtic maple. The tree is thought to have come to Britain in the Tudor period and was first recorded in 1632 in Kent. However, a tree thought to be the original British sycamore, the *fior chrann*, has been found to have grown in Scotland as far back as the late sixth and early seventh centuries.

Today, the sycamore is the most common native tree in Britain, central and eastern Europe and western Asia. Its range includes Albania, Austria, Belgium, Bulgaria, Czech Republic, Georgia, Germany, Greece, Hungary, Italy, Lithuania, Poland, Romania, southern Russia, Switzerland and the former

Yugoslavia. Around 1870 the sycamore was introduced into America. First planted in New York and New Jersey, it was later cultivated as a park or street tree in New England and the Mid-Atlantic states. So prolific is the sycamore in the 21st century, it is now considered to be an environmental weed in some parts of Australia and an invasive species in New Zealand, Norway, and some areas of the United Kingdom. It has a high saline content, so much so that it kills all vegetation that might try to grow under it, and its leaf litter contains so much salt that it doesn't burn.

Despite mixed reviews, the sycamore has played its own unique role in British history where it has always been considered a protective tree in folklore. It was beneath a sycamore tree at Tolpuddle in Dorset that six agricultural labourers, known as the Tolpuddle Martyrs, formed an early trades union in 1834. They were found to have breached the Incitement to Mutiny Act 1797 and were extradited to Australia. The oritinal tree survived and is cared for today by the National Trust.

One ancient sycamore with distinctive yellow foliage formerly stood in the village of Corstorphine, now a suburb of Edinburgh, Scotland. Not only was it claimed to be the 'largest sycamore in Scotland' but also the scene of James Lord Forrester's murder in 1679. The tree was blown down in a storm almost twenty years ago, but a replacement, grown from a cutting, now stands in the churchyard of Corstorphine Kirk. Another renowned sycamore near the Newbattle Abbey near Dalkeith, planted in 1550, was the specimen with the earliest known planting date in Scotland. It had achieved a girth of five m and a height of twenty-six metres by the time it was toppled by a gale in May 2006 at the grand old age of 456 years.

'The Holy Sycamore of Matarea', taken from
Jerusalem und das Heilige Land, by Johann Nepomuk, 1863.

TAMARISK

THE SEVENTEENTH-CENTURY herbalist, Nicholas Culpeper, wrote 'THE TAMARISK NEVER grows to be a tree of any great bigness in England, though beyond the seas it will; having a rough dark brown bark. The younger branches are of a chestnut colour, clothed with very fine tender green leaves, somewhat like those of cypress, but thinner and finer, and not at all hard or rough; the flowers grow in rough spikes at the ends of the younger shoots, an inch or more in length, several spikes growing together, each consisting of a great many small, five leaved, pale red flowers, which are succeeded by small seed, included in a downy substance.' Culpeper believed that the tree originated from Spain because it was believed that the word tamarisk, from the Latin tamarix, originally referred to the Tamaris River in the region that is now Spain.

Said to have been a favourite of the Greek God Apollo, the tamarisk has been the stuff of legend since antiquity. In ancient Egypt the body of Osiris was hidden beneath a tamarisk until it was retrieved by Isis. In the Mesopotamian epic poem Gilgamesh it was written that the Goddess Ninsun bathed in a bath of tamarisk and soapwort. In the Bible Abraham planted a tamarisk. And in the Qur'an the people of Saba were punished when Allah converted their gardens with plants that gave bitter fruit and tamarisks.

The Bible tells of *The Treaty at Beersheba* in which Abraham plants tamarisk trees. Beersheba is the only place that the Bible recorded Abraham planting trees and still today there is still an ancient well located at at this site called Abraham's well and tamarisk trees grow in the area. Most botanists and religious scholars are unanimous in their agreement that the trees that Abraham planted were the *Tamarix aphylla*, also known as the athel pine, and athel tree.

Tamarisk trees are certainly unusual in that they produce a substance called manna, although there is some debate as to whether this is produced by the tree in response to attacks by insects, or whether the sticky sweet substance is produced by the insects. Some say the tree is the source of the Biblical manna that the Israelites of the Bible were sent by God, although scholars refute this. What is certain is that the manna, galls from the trees and the wood have been used in medicine in a variety of countries. The Tuareg In Niger use manna to sweeten water.

The French tamarisk has been used for its astringent qualities, and notably the galls contain 40 per cent tannin, so it has been used to clean wounds, treat diarrhoea and dysentery, to staunch the flow of blood from wounds and speed up the healing process. It has anti-inflammatory properties, as traditionally it has been used for centuries to relieve pain and swelling. A decoction of the bark was used for eczema and other skin complaints. Used internally an infusion is said to boost the immune system, ward off colds and flu and other infections. Extracts from the tree are also an ingredient in traditional wart remedies in Italy, and in other parts of Europe it was a remedy for ridding the gastro-intestinal tract of worms.

TEA

WHEN CAPTAIN COOK landed in New South Wales, Australia in 1770, he learned about the tree the local aborigines named the 'healing tree'. The legend of the tree had been passed down for thousands of years by the indigenous Bundjalung tribes to treat coughs, colds and wounds with leaves. The Bundjalung believed in a magical coastal lake where leaves from trees had been falling into the water for hundreds of years and this had turned the lakes into medicinal baths. After allowing his crew to swim in the lake, wounds, cuts, scalds and other skin irritations were healed. The colour of the water, reminded Captain Cook of tea, and henceforth, the story goes, the tree was christened the tea tree.

The tea tree, *Melaleuca alternifolia*, is actually a small tree in the myrtle family, with sprawling leaves and feathery, fluffy white flowers, best suited to swampy flats and along the banks of streams. Shamans have used it for centuries to treat skin problems by adding crushed leaves into hot compresses and poultices. The healers were men, but the work of collecting the foliage and preparing it was that of the elder women, who placed them over a fire for a patient to inhale their steam or who made an infusion from them.

During the Second World War the Australian Army obtained possession of all income from tea tree oil to treat injured soldiers, and production of oil was considered an essential war time industry. Leaf-cutters in the plantations were exempt from military service, and although the supply of oil was limited, all soldiers had a small bottle of tea tree oil in their packs. The oil was especially important when battling in the jungle where mosquitoes and other blood-sucking insects were a hazard. Wounds, cuts and insect bites were treated with oil and the antiseptic properties eased discomfort and brought healing, with the risk of infection significantly diminished.

After Cook's discovery the tree was soon almost forgotten in the West. It was not until 1923 that Australian chemist Arthur Penfold discovered that the antiseptic action of the tea tree oil was around twelve times stronger than the then widely used carbolic acid. Subsequent scientific studies in London and Sydney showed that the oil to be an almost perfect antiseptic.

Commercial tea tree oil production developed soon after, with trees cut down by hand and their leaves often distilled on the spot in makeshift wood-fired bush stills. But it was not until the 1970s and 80s that large-scale production of tea tree oil took place. Today the anticeptic oil of the tea tree is in demand internationally and has become part of the mainstream.

WALNUT

WALNUTS HAVE BEEN discovered in the ancient Shanidar caves in northern Iraq and in a Mesolithic dunghill in Switzerland dating to the Neolithic period, from between 6,000 to 2,000 BCE. Mesopotamia, the area that is now modern Iraq, boasted of walnut groves in the famed Hanging Gardens of Babylon about 2,000 BCE. The Chaldeans left clay tablet inscriptions that accounted for these orchards and these are the earliest written records mentioning walnuts.

From Medieval times up until the end of the 18th century, Europeans were blanching, crushing, and soaking walnuts and almonds to create a rich, nutritious milk, a common household staple. While the poor dined on the wild walnuts, the rich were able to afford the larger, more expensive, cultivated variety.

Toward the end of the 17th century, walnuts along with chestnuts became important staples in France. During the famine of 1663 the poor consumed their walnuts and then resorted to grinding up the shells along with acorns to create coarse, unpalatable bread.

In the Second World War when families living in the small villages of Perigord, a region in the southern part of France, had little to eat, they turned to their walnut groves for a source of protein, whilst in North America native Indians enjoyed the pleasures and health benefits of the black walnut well before European explorers arrived.

The English walnut, *Juglans regia*, has been in Britain since the time of the Romans, who are credited with spreading the tree through most of Europe. These islands were at the northern edge of the tree's range, lacking enough warmth and sun to promote the best harvest of nuts and timber.

The word *juglans*, from the Latin, means 'the royal acorn of Jupiter.'

Because the walnut shell has an appearance reminiscent of the human brain, the Afghanistani word for walnut is *charmarghz* or 'four brains'. The tree's other name – Persian walnut – gives a better clue to its origins.

The tree was only later called the English walnut to distinguish it from the American variety, known as Black walnut, *Juglans nigra*. It grows to around thirty metres with a trunk two metres in diameter.

The rich colours of walnut became fashionable in the late 17th century when English oak was ousted as the hallmark of the best quality furniture. The complex grain patterns that make the wood so distinctive come from the bole of the trunk nearest the ground that is harvested from a large mature tree.

The walnut vogue only lasted around fifty years. In 1709 a bitter winter killed about two-thirds of all the mature walnut trees in Northern Europe. In 1720, alarmed by the rapid disappearance of their prized walnut trees, the French banned all export of the wood and the English were forced to substitute mahogany. Despite the tree's name the main area of supply for the English furniture trade was from the French Savoie region, and known as Grenoble walnut.

The early colonists carried seeds of the English walnut to the New World and planted them where they settled in Massachusetts and Virginia. However, the trees did not adapt easily to their new climate and could not even survive long enough to bear fruit. Black walnuts, however, were plentiful and soon became a valued ingredient in cookies and confections.

In the early 1800's Spanish Franciscan monks settled along the California coast. Part of their teachings included the cultivation of food plants and trees in the areas surrounding the missions. One area that eventually became the city of Walnut, California, was home to the San Gabriel Mission named for the Gabrielino Indians, originally of Shoshone origin. Many acres of walnut trees, originally brought from Spain, were planted here and became known as mission walnuts.

Some growers warn that walnut trees can be damaged by severe frosts but all the evidence is that they are now thriving. Grey squirrels in England have taken to stealing the nuts, burying them, and creating new walnut woodlands. One possible drawback to the trees is that they have a dense canopy and the roots release chemicals into the soil, which inhibits other plants growing around them – so walnuts need plenty of space.

Shorter winters and more sunshine are providing perfect growing and fruiting conditions for walnut trees. Some nurseries are offering as many as twenty varieties of walnut, some for the quality of their nuts and some for timber or ornament.

WILLOW

THE LEAVES AND bark of the willow tree have been mentioned in ancient Egyptian manuscripts as a remedy for aches and fevers and in the fifth century AD the Greek physician Hippocrates wrote about its medicinal properties in the fifth century BC.

Some of humans' earliest manufactured items may have been made from willow. A fishing net made from willow dates back to 8300 BC. Baskets, wattle fences and house walls were often woven from osiers or willow shoots. One of the forms of Welsh coracle traditionally uses willow. Thin or split willow rods can be woven into wicker, since it is less likely to split while being woven than many other woods, and can be bent around sharp corners in basketry.

Willow wood is also used in the manufacture cricket bats, grown from certain strains of white willow, cradle boards and furniture. The wood is used to make paper, string and rope. Willow is also used in the manufacture of double basses for backs, sides and linings, and in making splines and blocks for bass repair.

The willow is a famous subject in many cultures in Eastern Asia, and features in pen and ink paintings from China and Japan. In Japanese tradition, the willow is associated with ghosts. It is popularly supposed that a ghost will appear where a willow grows. Willow trees are also quite prevalent in folklore and myths.

In China, some people carry willow branches with them on the day of their Tomb Sweeping Qingming festival. Willow branches are also put up on gates and/or front doors, which they believe help ward off the evil spirits that wander on Qingming. Guanyin, the goddess of mercy, is often depicted sitting on a rock with a willow branch in a vase of water at her side.

In English folklore, a willow tree is believed to be sinister, capable of uprooting itself and stalking travellers.

'White heron beneath willow tree', by Shinsai Ryuryukyo, 1805.

YEW

Old Yew, which graspest at the stones
That name the under-lying dead,
Thy fibers net the dreamless head,
Thy roots are wrapt about the bones.

WHEN ALFRED LORD Tennyson wrote of the yew in his poem *In Memoriam* he drew upon the metaphor of the roots tree to describe the intense grief of lost love when his friend Henry Hallam died suddenly from a brain hemorrhage in 1833.

Long before the eighteenth century the European yew, *Taxus baccata,* had been considered a gloomy, sinister tree, planted in graveyards and around churches, although many scholars argue that old yews were to be found near Christian churches first. The buildings simply took over ancient sacred sites.

Legend held that whoever fell asleep under the shade of a yew would die. Robert Turner in his book *Botanoaotia* written in 1636 was damning of the yew. 'If the yew be set in a place subject to poisonous vapours, the very branches will draw and imbibe them'. And in William Shakespeare's Macbeth, witches stir a cauldron containing 'slips of yew'.

Yet in many cultures the yew symbolizes not death, but renewal and a transcendence of mortality. Along with other evergreens, the tree has always been considered holy because of its ability to retain its leaves and to split under the weight of advanced growth without rendering itself vulnerable to disease or infestation.

To the Celts the yew was associated with noble sacrifice. Indeed, Julius Caesar wrote in his Gallic Wars that Caturoleus, chief of the Eburones, poisoned himself with a poison made from the toxic leaves and bark of the yew rather than surrender to Rome. The botanical name of the yew is *Taxus* and the Greek poison smeared on arrows used in battle was *toxicon*, a substance that scholars believe may have contained yew.

Yew wood is strong and flexible and in the Middle Ages this made it ideal for musical instruments such as lutes, but it was in armory that yew was prized over all other woods. For centuries bows and longbows were made of yew. In *Chaucer's Canterbury Tales* an archer is described as a 'yewman'. During the sixteenth century muskets became the weapon of choice, partly due to the decline in yew trees. During this period many were felled and not replaced.

Every part of the yew is poisonous, except the berries. Despite this, in the eleventh century AD Avicenna prescribed compounds of yew bark as a cure for heart ailments. In Asia an extract made from yew bark has been believed by traditional herbalists to cure breast cancer.

Nowadays many ancient yews are protected. Hopefully, their melancholic reputation will be put to one side. They are great trees just as they are part of our history. As John Evelyn, in his *Sylva: A Discourse of Forest Trees* wrote in 1664, being surrounded by woods of eye someone 'might without the least violence to his imagination easily fancy himself transported into some new or enchanted country.

BIBLIOGRAPHY

The Wisdom of Trees, by Max Adams, Head of Zeus, 2014

The Correspondence of John Bartram, edited by Edmund and Dorothy Smith Berkeley, University Press of Florida, 1992

Travels of William Bartram, edited by Mark van Doren, Dover, 1928

The Compleat Naturalist: a Life of Linnaeus, by Wilfrid Blunt, Princeton University Press, 1992

The Origins of Plants, by Maggie Campbell-Colver, Headline, 2005

Dangerous Tastes, by Andrew Dalby

New Voyage around the World, by William Dampier, Dover

Abbe David's Diary, Abbe David Armand, Harvard University Press

The Plant-Lore and Garden-Craft of Shakespeare, by Henry N Ellacombe, Edward Arnold, 1896

The Meaning of Trees, by Fred Hageneder, Chronicle, 2003

Britain's Tree Story, by Julian Hight, National Trust Books, 2011

Thomas Jefferson's Garden Book, by Thomas Jefferson, American Philosophical Society, 1944

Ancient Trees, by Anna Lewington and Edward Parker, Collins and Brown, 1999

Flora Britannica, by Richard Mabey, Chatto, 1997

Hidden Trees of Britain, by Archie Miles, Ebury, 2007

Plants of the Bible, by Harold N Moldenke and L Alma, Dover, 1952

Ancient Trees: Portraits of Time, by Beth Moon, Abbeville, 2014

An Empire of Plants, by Toby and Will Musgrave, Cassell, 2000

Meetings with Remarkable Trees, Thomas Pakenham, Phoenix, 2001

Tree Wisdom, by Jacqueline Memory Paterson, Thorsons, 2011

Trees in Nature, Myth and Art, by Ernest Phythian, Methuen, 1907

The Last Forest, by Professor Oliver Rackham, Dent Books, 1989

The Long, long Life of Trees, by Fiona Stafford, Yale University Press, 2016

The Heritage Trees of Britain and Northern Ireland, by John Stokes, Constable, 2004

Dangerous Garden, by David Stuart, Francis Lincoln, 2004

The History of Gardens, by Christopher Thacker

The Secret Life of Trees, by Colin Tudge, Penguin, 2006

Leaves in Myth, Magic and Medicine, by Alice Thomas Vitale

The Hidden Life of Trees, by Peter Wohlleben, Greystone, 2016

INDEX